JOSEPH

A LIFE OF PROVIDENCE, INJUSTICE, AND FORGIVENESS

BRIAN BAILEY

EVP
EARTHEN VESSEL PUBLISHING

JOSEPH: A LIFE OF PROVIDENCE, INJUSTICE, AND
FORGIVENESS

ISBN: 978-0-9907277-6-7 (First Edition, 2015)
Earthen Vessel Publishing
San Rafael, CA

DEDICATION

For my friend and honorary sister, Robin, who, like Joseph, has forgiven much.

Contents

INTRODUCTION

Were it literature alone, there would be no grander, more enduring family epic than the family narrative found in Genesis spanning the lives of Abram to Joseph. It is the founding of the premier nation and ethnic group in history. James Michener, for all of his story telling genius, could never approach its brilliance. But this is not fiction, some mythology of a nomadic people; this is history contained in the divinely inspired Scripture. This narrative has a purpose for us today, four thousand years removed from the events. "For whatever was written in former days was written for our instruction, that through endurance and through the encouragement of the Scriptures we might have hope." (Romans 15:4)

As much as we learn of the character and nature of this fledgling Hebrew nation, we also learn of the mysterious, omnipotent God who intervenes in their lives. We see them seemingly plucked from obscurity and placed on their dynamic journey through history. Indeed as God told Abram, "...through you all nations of the earth shall be blessed..." (Genesis 12:3)

We will focus our attention on the end of the Genesis narrative with Joseph, the great-grandson of Abram. Why Joseph? Jo-

1

seph shared common life experiences to which we can relate on various levels even in our day. We study the life of Joseph because he suffered affliction as we all will or have suffered in our lives.

Affliction seems to come at us from essentially one of two directions: either those stemming from the fallen nature of the natural world in which we live (death, disease, pestilence, and natural disaster) or from evil at the hands of human agents. In the book of Ruth we see people who respond to forces of nature that devastate their lives. In the story of Joseph, we see a man who is devastated not by forces of nature, by disease, but by the animus of family, the spiteful hatred of a spurned would-be lover, and the careless forgetfulness of a new acquaintance. The questions are raised: How do God's people properly respond to the evil acts of others against them? Also, what part does God and His will play in all of these events? Do we believe, as deists, that God created the world and merely acts as a spectator to see how it shall all end, or is He actively engaged in the lives of His people? Or put another way: is the hand of God involved in our affliction? What we will see is the hand of God actively involved in all of these events that Joseph experienced, those we call "good" and those we humanly call "evil".

We study the life of Joseph, because he suffered injustice at the hands of others. The dynamic of the family life- his interaction with the ten brothers shaped everything. The hatred directed toward Joseph is a most integral part of this narrative. Injustice is a man-made condition as there is no injustice with God. With man injustice is rampant. We as believers can neither pretend it does not exist nor sweep it under the rug. In the Bible we see injustice condemned. The impetus for justice is no further than Jesus' injunction to treat others as we ourselves would desire to be treated. Justice and righteousness are co-joined.

Lastly, we study the life of Joseph, because although we may never confront injustice on any major scale in our own lives, we will confront the issue of forgiveness towards others. Even we, the redeemed, sin against and hurt those around us on some level.

Offense often seems to be an issue of proximity. Those closest to us bear the weight of our sinful imperfections and choices, as we do theirs. Forgiveness is the necessary and vital lubricant for the machinery of all human relationships. We cannot relate to others unless we learn to forgive their offenses and they ours. The need for forgiveness is as old as mankind. King Solomon proclaimed in Ecclesiastes, "There is nothing new under the sun..." (Ecclesiastes 1:9-10) The life of Joseph, his brothers and his father will make this point with tremendous eloquence.

The book is divided among the lines of Providence, Injustice and Forgiveness. The division is something of a misnomer. This division of these three themes is not by any measure equal, and it is erroneous to consider them three distinct parts.

To use a visual illustration, we might think of the material this way:

PROVIDENCE   INJUSTICE   FORGIVENESS
Joseph

Perhaps a better thought is to consider it this way:

PROVIDENCE
INJUSTICE   FORGIVENESS
Joseph

Our point is that Providence overshadows everything, every facet of Joseph's life. Providence is all about God, and Joseph's story is all about God. All of this is about God's glory. The Westminster Catechism instructs us that we are created for God's glory. As we will see, Joseph's life glorified God.

PROLOGUE

SHECHEM

As for the bones of Joseph, which the people of Israel brought up from Egypt, they buried them at Shechem, in the piece of land that Jacob bought from the sons of Hamor the father of Shechem for a hundred pieces of money. It became an inheritance of the descendants of Joseph. (Joshua 24:32)

I t was a solemn occasion in the history of Israel. On this day a promise made to a patriarch over four hundred years before was being honored. Joseph's bones, brought from Egypt in the exodus were being interred in Shechem.

We read in the last chapter in the book of Genesis final events in the life of Joseph:

And Joseph said to his brothers, "I am about to die, but God will visit you and bring you up out of this land to the land that he swore to Abraham, to Isaac, and to Jacob." Then Joseph made the sons of Israel swear, saying, "God will surely visit you, and you shall carry up my bones from here." So Joseph died, being 110 years old. They embalmed him, and he was put in a coffin in Egypt. (Genesis 50: 24-26)

These final words call for a future event, from a man whom God had gifted with perceiving the future from dreams. Joseph's words for his people were words of hope, words of promise. Egypt was not their earthly home; no, the Hebrews had a far country promised to Joseph's great-grandfather Abraham. Over the course of four centuries, the dream of Joseph seemed to dim as his descendents suffered the indignities of slavery and oppression but, curiously, some among them remembered Joseph's dream and kept his mortal remains for that glorious future.

So now he is to be buried in Shechem. What an interesting turn of events. Life and death have come full circle. You see, wandering around in the area of Shechem, all of those years ago as a seventeen-year-old youth, looking for his brothers is where a great and difficult journey started.

But we are getting ahead of ourselves in the narrative.

CHAPTER ONE

WE ARE NOT DEISTS

It is tempting when we study and exegete Joseph's life to start in Genesis chapter 37.

We cannot truly start there. Our beginning is to examine a supposition about God and humankind. That supposition is that God is completely involved with humankind on a most intimate level. If we do not remember this fact then we will not fully grasp all that Joseph's life has to teach us about our own. God's reach into the individual self is breath-taking:

> LORD, you have examined me and you know me. You know everything I do; from far away you understand all my thoughts. You see me, whether I am working or resting; you know all my actions. Even before I speak, you already know what I will say. You are all around me on every side; you protect me with your power. Your knowledge of me is too deep; it is beyond my understanding. Where could I go to escape from you? Where could I get away from your presence? If I went up to heaven, you would be there; if I lay down in the world of the dead, you would be there. If I flew away beyond the east or lived in the farthest place... you

would be there to lead me, you would be there to help me. I could ask the darkness to hide me or the light around me to turn into night, but even darkness is not dark for you, and the night is as bright as the day. Darkness and light are the same to you. You created every part of me; you put me together in my mother's womb. I praise you because you are to be feared; all you do is strange and wonderful. I know it with all my heart. When my bones were being formed, carefully put together in my mother's womb, when I was growing there in secret, you knew that I was there—you saw me before I was born. The days allotted to me had all been recorded in your book, before any of them ever began. O God, how difficult I find your thoughts; how many of them there are! If I counted them, they would be more than the grains of sand. When I awake, I am still with you. (Psalms 139, Good News Translation)

This knowledge is frightening and comforting. It is frightening to the degree that He sees our broken sinfulness. His piercing eye does see all of our sinful failures and shameful self-will. So often we make our own beds in our own earthly, self-created hell. Our self-deception bears bitter fruit. Adam and Eve hid in the Garden filled with shame and fear and we do the same. God's desire is to love us and this knowledge of His total perception of us provides comfort. The rift in the Garden was healed with the blood of the cross. The great desire of the human heart is to both completely (as much as any mere human can) know another and be known, and still be loved and accepted. This concept explains more completely, the concept of 'knowing' as it relates to husbands and wives. It is that loving and being loved that is far more than mere biological sex, it is emotional, it is spiritual, it is a union always of...grace.

We were created for a level of intimacy with Yahweh as well. Simple religion might present facts about God or His word. Knowing God, in the same vein as spouses, on the emotional and spiritual level, is a far different thing than grasping a theological framework or memorizing a spate of Bible verses. Grasping a framework and knowing Scripture word for word is important but does not begin to scratch the surface of knowing God.

Psalm 139 explains clearly that Yahweh truly knows us—everything about us in full total. Joseph lived this truth to its' fullest extent although he may not have fully grasped it: God knew everything about Joseph's life and He was involved in the details. A common phrase is that the devil is in the details. No, as we will see in our study of Joseph--GOD is in the details.

So, we are not deists.

We do not believe that God wound the world up as a giant top and pulled the string, watching it spin off into the universe. There is the testimony in Psalms and there is the story of Joseph himself that shows the constant care and action of a fully involved, fully comprehending creator.

CHAPTER TWO

BEGINNINGS: ABRAHAM

Now the LORD said to Abram, "Go from your country and your kindred and your father's house to the land that I will show you. And I will make of you a great nation, and I will bless you and make your name great, so that you will be a blessing. I will bless those who bless you, and him who dishonors you I will curse, and in you all the families of the earth shall be blessed." So Abram went, as the LORD had told him, and Lot went with him. Abram was seventy-five years old when he departed from Haran. And Abram took Sarai his wife, and Lot his brother's son, and all their possessions that they had gathered, and the people that they had acquired in Haran, and they set out to go to the land of Canaan. Genesis 12: 1-5)

H ow staggering were Abram's actions—leaving ALL for a land yet unknown with promises huge in scope but limited in details. Probably more than one person questioned Abram's sanity to his face. "Leave an established civilization for what—a wilderness with few outposts?!" The explorers and settlers of North America understood these issues as well. Adventure calls with all of its requisite promises and risks.

As the world may see it, living a radical, Christ-dependent life is perhaps suspect, archaic, and narrow. It is Thoreau's different drummer magnified. A culture that prides itself on autonomy finds any dependence (especially on an unseen deity) unsettling, even scary. But then, that is what faith is all about, isn't it? Faith in Yahweh is placing ourselves in His grasp, willingly, and trusting the results to His good will. There is the element of adventure, of abandonment, of placing ourselves, from the world's eyes, at risk—trusting that we will not fall into oblivion.

Faith in God is typified by sitting down onto a chair, trusting that the chair will not collapse under our weight and deposit us on the floor, red-faced. You cannot truly be counted as having faith in the chair unless you lower your body to a point of no return as far as gravity is concerned. You must 'ask' the chair to hold your weight.

Abram's sitting in the chair, metaphorically speaking, was leaving for Canaan, leaving Haran and Ur behind. He asked God to hold his weight in following His call to an unknown, yet unseen land.

What is also instructive for us as we examine Abram's life is that in periods after God's great blessings, Abram would fail and fail miserably. Rather than trust God in these particular situations and rest in faith, trusting God for what he had said to Abram, he took counsel of his own fears. Yet God was gracious to Abram in spite of his lack of trust. Yes, Abram was tested and failed. His failure was of no surprise to God. The response of God in all of this is to show mercy and grace. God knows that we have times where trusting God seems beyond us, more than what we humanly think the circumstances warrant. We think we must step in and engineer a solution. We all have sought to help God out, to our own detriment. Yet for all of his failures, the arch of Abram's faith-life was upward. "And he (Abram) believed the LORD, and he counted it to him as righteousness" (Genesis 15:6).

Abram had a vision that defined the covenant promise to him from God, a covenant that declared emphatically that Abram will have many descendents.

This vision was critical for Abram because by this time in his life, being an aged man with an aged wife, he felt that such a promise was fantastic. Abram believed that he was as good as dead. But God came to him in the stillness of the night and made an incredible promise that Abram's heirs would number like the stars in the sky, far too many to comprehend and to count. "And he believed the Lord, and he counted it to him as righteousness." Abram responded in faith.[1]

This faith was passed down and Joseph is a key part of Abram's future—he is part of the greater multitude of promise. God initiated the covenant; God was the covenant giver. God himself made the promise that he will do great things in the life of Abram and the life of Abram's descendents.

Woven into the cloth of God's promises are dark threads; we see a hard prophecy of servitude.

> *Then the LORD said to Abram, "Know for certain that your offspring will be sojourners in a land that is not theirs and will be servants there, and they will be afflicted for four hundred years. But I will bring judgment on the nation that they serve, and afterward they shall come out with great possessions. As for you, you shall go to your fathers in peace; you shall be buried in a good old age. And they shall come back here in the fourth generation, for the iniquity of the Amorites is not yet complete." (Genesis 15: 13-15)*

This servitude was intertwined with the promise: the Hebrews would be, in large part, defined as who they were due to this troubled, painful history. As our pains and pleasures create and define who we are, so the slavery helped to create and define the national character of the Hebrews.

---

1   See Endnote *

The hardship that would be endured does not change the focus and scope of God's promise. Abram was told that God would
be his shield, and that of his heirs. God would shield them not
from times of trouble and difficulty but through those times of
difficulty. He promised Abram that his reward would be very
great and that his very own son would be his heir. Joseph's life
is symbolic of the Hebrew ethnic experiences: he is the favored
child who will endure a defining period of slavery.

Spiritually, we all were born into slavery. We were enslaved
to our sin by our rebellion against God. Our sin places us in
chains far stronger than any made with steel or iron. That slavery goes into the very depth, in the recesses, the very corners of
our soul. And this slavery to sin is lethal for Scripture tells us
very plainly that wages of sin are fatal.[2]

Joseph, once enslaved, was ultimately freed from slavery.
The Hebrew people, once enslaved, were also given their freedom. Jesus died on the cross and was resurrected that we, in
slavery to sin and bound to the limitations and frailties of the
human body and soul, might be freed from sin's dominion and
pervasive control over our lives.

ENDNOTES:

* That is why it depends on faith, in order that the promise may
rest on grace and be guaranteed to all his offspring—not only to the ad-
herent of the law but also to the one who shares the faith of Abraham,
who is the father of us all, as it is written, "I have made you the father
of many nations"—in the presence of the God in whom he believed,
who gives life to the dead and calls into existence the things that do
not exist. In hope he believed against hope, that he should become the
father of many nations, as he had been told, "So shall your offspring
be." He did not weaken in faith when he considered his own body,
which was as good as dead (since he was about a hundred years old),
or when he considered the barrenness of Sarah's womb. No unbelief
made him waver concerning the promise of God, but he grew strong

---

2   See Endnote **

in his faith as he gave glory to God, fully convinced that God was able to do what he had promised. That is why his faith was "counted to him as righteousness" (Romans 4:16-22).

** The iniquities of the wicked ensnare him, and he is held fast in the cords of his sin. (Proverbs 5: 22)

Jesus answered them, "Truly, truly, I say to you, everyone who practices sin is a slave to sin" (John 8:34).

We know that our old self was crucified with him in order that the body of sin might be brought to nothing, so that we would no longer be enslaved to sin. For one who has died has been set free from sin. Now if we have died with Christ, we believe that we will also live with him. We know that Christ, being raised from the dead, will never die again; death no longer has dominion over him. For the death he died he died to sin, once for all, but the life he lives he lives to God. So you also must consider yourselves dead to sin and alive to God in Christ Jesus. Let not sin therefore reign in your mortal body, to make you obey its passions. Do not present your members to sin as instruments for unrighteousness, but present yourselves to God as those who have been brought from death to life, and your members to God as instruments for righteousness. For sin will have no dominion over you, since you are not under law but under grace. What then? Are we to sin because we are not under law but under grace? By no means! Do you not know that if you present yourselves to anyone as obedient slaves, you are slaves of the one whom you obey, either of sin, which leads to death, or of obedience, which leads to righteousness? But thanks be to God, that you who were once slaves of sin have become obedient from the heart to the standard of teaching to which you were committed, and having been set free from sin, have become slaves of righteousness (Romans 6: 6-18).

The wages of sin is death, but the gift of God is eternal life through Jesus Christ our Lord (Romans 6:23).

CHAPTER THREE

BEGINNINGS: JACOB

I t is interesting to note that in both the life of Abram as well as his grandson Jacob, there is a promise given by God with what amounts to a substantial delay in its fulfillment. Abram, later to be called Abraham, waited twenty—five years for God to fulfill the promise of a birth heir.

Jacob, as well, waited a substantial period of time for the fulfillment of promises made to him when he was fleeing for his life from his brother, Esau. God's promise to Jacob was twofold: he would have many descendents and he would possess the land where he stood, a continuation of the promise to Abraham. In the particular case of descendents, Scripture records that Jacob sired twelve sons. It took Jacob twenty years of servitude to his father-in-law Laban before he was able to emancipate himself economically and return to the land promised to him by God. The second part of the promise would not be fulfilled until after the 400 year period of slavery in Egypt. The promise was fulfilled with the Exodus led by Moses and the settling of the land under the leadership of Joshua.

The Scriptures are, if nothing else, unflinching in their portrayal of its characters strengths and weaknesses. Jacob, Abraham's grandson, was no saint. In fact, Jacob was a liar and a thief. Jacob's father Isaac and Jacob's mother Rebecca each had a favored child. Isaac favored Esau and Rebecca favored Jacob. It appears in Scripture, found in Genesis chapter 27, that the theft of the fathers blessing was orchestrated by Rebecca. Given the dynamic of her birth family this comes as no great surprise. In Jacob's relationship with father-in-law, Laban, we will see the same conniving and deviousness turned on Jacob himself. It seems it as if God in fact does have a sense of humor.

Were we to meet Jacob as a young man on the streets today our wisest choice would be to hold onto our wallets while we shook hands. It is somewhat incredible to consider that the promise of God's blessings came to Jacob after terrible moral failures. But such is the grace of God and mercy of God. It is easy from our human standpoint to think of Jacob as most undeserving of any good thing from God. However, the Scriptures teach clearly that we are all morally broken, deficient and undeserving of any goodness from God.

Frozen in the moment, God's actions seem totally enigmatic. God would take the duplicitous Jacob and turn him into the wrestler who grappled with an angel (or perhaps the pre-incarnate Christ). We mortals are so tied to a space and time continuum, so much to the present, so much to the now that we lose sight of the fact that God sees the totality of life's parade. Grace is bound up, in so many ways, in that God looks at us, and sees not where we currently are, He sees where He's going to take us.

To utilize a New Testament example, if we look at Saul as we see him in Acts chapter 8 and the beginning of chapter 9, he presents as a dangerous, single-minded zealot. Saul could not see the Christian men, women, and children that he hounded and imprisoned as human beings; he saw them as blasphemers and heretics to be destroyed. Any believer would steer clear of him and stay out of sight as much as possible. This is precisely the issues that Ananias raised when he is told to go meet Saul after Saul's confrontation on the Damascus road. All Ananias knew is what this man had done, how Saul had made it his life's ambition and goal to destroy the nascent church. The response given to Ananias is that Saul has been chosen to carry the gospel to the Gentiles. God knew and saw where He was going to take Saul and the apostle he would become.

God is going to work in the life of Jacob but it will not be easy nor will it be quick. In the realm of spiritual growth and development this is true for all of us, as there is no easy road to growth and maturity. So often in our lives it seems as if God takes His time. To be sure, temporal circumstances can change in an instant. As we will see in the life of Joseph, God can also choose to move with a blinding speed that leaves us dazed.

God will use the passage of time in the life of Jacob to mold him and make him. It is a life long process for Jacob as it is for us all. None of us arrives in this life; we never come to a place of total spiritual completeness and maturity. We do not finish the spiritual process in this life. There will always be growth needed. So as we watch God's redemption in the lives of others, our hope is for growth in His timing, which may not be our timing or on our schedule. The invisible hand of God moves as God purposes.

It is easy to look at Jacob and malign his character. However, we can respect the character of Joseph. Who taught Joseph? We can only conclude that for all of Jacob's faults, God graciously allowed him to pass the faith on to Joseph and we can only assume that by the time Jacob parented Joseph, he did pass on good aspects of character to him.

CHAPTER FOUR

BEGINNINGS: JOSEPH

Joseph, the son of Jacob. Jacob, the son of Isaac. Isaac, the son of Abraham.

We are, in many ways, the sum of our ancestors, often a mixture of their noble and base traits and character. None of us escape the imprint of these past lives on our personalities and psyche. We claim individuality almost to the exclusion of all else, but our family that proceeds us wields a unique power to bless or curse our lives.

In a relative sense, most of us are on a sliding scale between good and evil. Reformed or Calvinistic theology deems us as in *total depravity* and we are not denying that here. No, we are looking at people as they compare to others in society as opposed to the strict theological sense. We see that there is a whole spectrum of behavior and attitudes that range from utterly evil to reasonably good. As we examine the lives of Abraham, Isaac, and Jacob, they were essentially men with redeeming character values yet, as previously mentioned, we also read in the text that they were flawed individuals. These character flaws were passed down into the growing Jacob family and all of this would ultimately create havoc and suffering in the life of young Joseph.

As we have said, to understand the character of Joseph and that of his immediate family you have to go back to the beginning of the clan with Abraham. Abraham was a man who at times exhibited exemplary faith, and at other times exhibited shameful fear and mistrust. If we're not careful fear can define us and color our decisions and actions. Abraham feared that the beauty of his wife Sarah would be his undoing and untimely death at the hand of the Egyptians. These events were within a short period after God had appeared to him and told him to leave his homeland and travel to Canaan. Just as Jacob would send his sons, due to famine, into Egypt, so Abram traveled to Egypt, because of famine. While there, he became convinced that his wife would be taken by force and he slain. Forgetting the clear promise of God Abram used a half-truth to protect himself while simultaneously placing Sarah in great peril. Years later Abraham repeated the same scenario from Egypt with King Abimelech.

So we see that Abraham was not above lying to save his own skin. Although positive aspects of Abraham's faith passed down to Joseph and became the fabric of this young man's life, Abraham's situational dishonesty created a behavior template in the family that crashed into Joseph's life with devastating force.

Isaac matured into essentially a good man but he had one major fault: he showed favoritism to one son (Esau) over the other (Jacob). Isaac's wife, Rebecca, schemed to show favoritism to Jacob. When she saw an opportunity, she schemed with Jacob to supplant Esau and take leadership of the clan. Young Jacob was a cunning, oily, snake. He feared his brother Esau for good reason: Jacob connived Esau out of his birthright and stole his father's deathbed blessing. For this deception Esau was ready to murder his brother. Of course, Jacob will meet his match in future father-in-law, Laban in conniving. Jacob, not learning the lesson of favoritism's bane, will show favoritism to the children of Rachel at the expense of the other children.

It is the grace of this eternal God we serve that He graciously blesses our weak, inadequate efforts. His grace goes beyond our sin to produce his fruits in our lives. Our sin, however, not only scars our life but the lives of those we love, even to future generations. There is truly no victimless sin. Jacob changed over time, but his own sins impacted his children and wives.

There is no reason to think that the other sons of Jacob did not know Jacob's history and doubtless feared they would be passed over for Joseph. The family dynamic of the willingness to lie and choose favorites resulted in Jacob placing Joseph in an exalted position he, by birthright, should never have held. This favoritism and Joseph's youthful pride opened the road to hatred from the other brothers. Joseph was such a thorn to the brothers that they could not even share a peaceful meal with Joseph. That hatred resulted in a cruel betrayal and a heartless lie to cover up the treachery toward their younger half-brother.

Joseph, because of a youthful lack of discretion, didn't help himself by telling of his dreams. The sins of the fathers are visited on their children. Jacob had sinned against his father and brother through deceit. The ten sons of Jacob sinned against Jacob and Joseph and committed a heinous deceit. It was murder really, for in their hearts they knew Joseph could die a slave in another land.

For all of their flaws and sins, these men, Abraham, Isaac, and Jacob produced an incredible immediate spiritual lineage. Joseph was imprinted with their great faith and sense of responsibility to Yahweh. This young man found his faith, not in a moment of crisis, in chains, going to Egypt but rather at the side of his father at a campfire. Doubtless Jacob had followed the injunction that Moses would pass down,

> *Israel, listen! Our God is the LORD! Only the LORD! Love the LORD your God with all your heart, all your being, and all your strength. These words that I am commanding you today must always be on your minds. Recite them to your children. Talk about them when you are sitting around your house and when you are out and about, when*

you are lying down and when you are getting up. Tie them
on your hand as a sign. They should be on your forehead as
a symbol. Write them on your house's doorframes and on
your city's gates. (Deuteronomy 6:4-9)

The point is that the faith is transferred like a runner's baton in a relay race. Now, the example is not perfect because we must keep our own faith, but the point is that there must be both a consistent life example and active, intentional, instruction. The common idea, "Let children decide for themselves when they are of age," is the basest form of child abuse because it neglects their eternal soul. If Jacob had taken this instructional track of some modern parents, Joseph would have never had the basis in faith that kept him out of Potiphar's wife's bed. We must be taught.

Jacob instructed Joseph: he gave him a strong foundation that cemented Joseph's sense of identity as a follower of Yahweh. Joseph knew he was accountable to the God of his father for every action he took.

Joseph at the onset of our story saw the clan history and family dynamics play out painfully in his life. But Joseph responded with faith rather than hatred and anger. In part because he was betrayed, he would not betray his God with Potiphar's wife. Under Potiphar he learned hard work and administration. In prison, his administrative skills were further honed as well as his ability to interpret dreams. He also learned the logical consequence of every crime and sin in the prison. His family's negative history did cause him suffering, but he rose above it.

CHAPTER FIVE

THE DIVINE DECREE, PROVIDENCE

There are some things that the LORD our God has kept secret; but he has revealed his Law, and we and our descendants are to obey it forever. Good News Translation (Deuteronomy 29:29 GNT)

When this writer was a teenager, he checked out a book from the library on film history and film production. The book itself was actually quite dated, back into the 1940s when the predominance of films produced were made in black and white. The information was fascinating. The major fact detailed in the book was that film, and by extension now television production, was radically different than the production of a play on the stage. Films and television are shot, not chronologically as far as the story goes by scene. The use of sets and locations becomes the primary consideration as far as what scenes are shot when. Consequently, as far as the filming schedule is concerned, actual filming can begin in the middle or even the end of the story itself. Although the actual filming may be out of sequence, there is a script, a storyline that ties all of the disparate scenes together.

We are examining the concept of God's decree, somewhat

out of sequence of the narrative, just like in film production, because the issue of how God works in history is absolutely crucial in our understanding of Joseph and all of the events of his life. Joseph's life was high drama with betrayal, suffering, injustice, and triumph.

Exactly what part does God play in all of these events? In an analogy from cinema, God is the producer and the director. Even that illustration falls woefully short of the truth and doing real justice to the reality, but you get some grasp of the idea.

The role of God in the events of Joseph's life is critical because by extension we wonder, what part does God play in the narrative and the history of our lives? Is God involved and does He rule in the totality of man's existence and his decisions, or is God merely a passive and silent bystander? In film parlance, is God truly the producer/director or is he the camera operator? Is man totally free in his will and intentions, with God providing moral direction and oversight, utilizing man's free will for His own divine purposes? How free are we truly, morally and in our ultimate choices? Can we thwart God's divine decree and stymie God's plan? Frankly, some of what we query here is beyond the scope of this book.

What we will see in this narrative of Joseph's life is that God is completely involved. He moves in the events that impacted Joseph. Yahweh-God is sovereign and He uses the choices, even of those bent on evil, for His good and wise will. In short, God takes the roll of producer, director, editor, and camera operator.

If we're going to understand what is going on in any of the events of the lives of the biblical characters and our lives, we must examine all of these events in the light and consideration of the rest of the Scriptures. When we want to form a deep, detailed theology, the tendency we must fight tooth and nail is that tendency to look at God and the things of God from the vantage point strictly of our human wisdom, understanding, and experience. We must fight this tendency because there is a disparity between what many in our current day think about God and his dealings in history and what the Scriptures themselves actually say about how God moves, acts, and interacts in history.

Herein lies the primary issue: the totality of Scripture is very clear when it comes to creation, when it comes to history, when it comes to nations and when it comes to our individual lives, God is the sovereign ruler and potentate of everything. Creation, history, nations and our individual lives are ruled by a wise Creator and nothing is left to chance.

What we are referring to here is the biblical doctrine of God's sovereignty and by extension God's decrees. In every facet of biblical literature, when we look at biblical history, when we look at the prophets, the wisdom literature, the narratives of the New Testament and the theology presented in the various letters, sovereignty is seeped in every area, every bit of Scripture. All of Scripture is the proving-ground, the display of God's sovereignty.

Nothing is left to chance?

For me, the writer, this discussion of God's sovereignty is not merely an intellectual-theological issue to be parsed. No, the impact of the concept is far more personal, far more profoundly meaningful. In the late summer of 1989, my nine-year-old son Charles was riding home from school with his mother when their car was struck by another, killing Charles instantly. In the summer of 2000, I was driving home after work when I was involved in an accident, my truck was hit on the driver's side. Looking at my accident, if my truck had been traveling a second faster the door panel would have been the locus of the collision and not the front left-side wheel well. That fact probably saved my life. If the car Charles was riding in was a second or two slower it is possible he may have survived. This, of course, being conjecture on my part as to the possible outcome.

Why was Charles taken; why was I spared? Why did those scant seconds, the time to take a breath, transpire as they did? Of course, on this side of life I do not know the ultimate answer to the why of it. I do know, I do trust that God was on His throne, sovereign, in 1989 just was He was in 2000. I trust that He ruled and overruled in both events, that He is good and does what is right even when it is, in my humanity, hard and painful. The loss of a child is among life's most painful losses, but I trust God and I trust I will see Charles again. I trust God was in these events. In all of this, I cling to the rock of God's good and wise sovereign rule.

Bruce Ware writes, "From the beginning of the Bible to the end (quite literally), readers are constantly encouraged, in account after account, to think of God as in control of what takes place in this world."[1]

Ware's assertion and understanding of the Bible is where we must begin in consideration of Joseph. What happened in Joseph's life is not chance, random events, or even what the Greeks would have called 'fate'.

In educational circles there is an ongoing debate, as far as the sciences, between the assertions of evolution as opposed to what is commonly called intelligent design. We would say that when it comes to history, in particular the life of Joseph, there was in fact an intelligent design behind all of these events.

Put simply, God planned for all of the events to transpire fulfilling a goal and purpose that He had in mind. As it relates to sovereignty what we are claiming here is that these events were fixed and set; they were not dependent upon any one person or persons. God's will and plan cannot and will not be thwarted by anything or anyone.

God decreed all of the events, what we would humanly call good and bad, in Joseph's life.

What do we mean when we talk about God making a decree for these events to transpire, for God to decree events? We do need to talk about this theologically because this whole theological concept of God's decrees is a linchpin for everything that will follow. At this point we will examine what saints from another

---

1   Bruce A. Ware, *God's Greater Glory: The Exalted God of Scripture and the Christian Faith* (Wheaton, IL: Crossway, 2004), 67.

era explained when they wrote the Westminster Confession of Faith. The Westminster Confession is the foundational document for Biblical Presbyterianism and what is commonly called reformed theology. This is how the Confession explains God's decrees:

> God from all eternity, did, by the most wise and holy counsel of His own will, freely, and unchangeably ordain whatsoever comes to pass; yet so, as thereby neither is God the author of sin, nor is violence offered to the will of the creatures; nor is the liberty or contingency of second causes taken away, but rather established. (Westminster Confession of Faith Chapter 3 Section 1)

Simply put, if it happens, God ordained it. If you have suffered, it can be staggering and beyond comprehension that a hard or terrible event in your life may have its genus in the mind of God. If I take seriously the teachings of scripture and consider the collective theological wisdom of the men who wrote the Westminster Confession, I have no other position to take than the position that God does decree suffering for our lives. As in my earlier personal example, God decreed Charles's death but my survival in two separate automobile accidents.

What we're saying here specifically about Joseph is that God did decree in eternity past that Joseph would be born into essentially a blended family, that he would be favored by his father and engender animus from his ten half-brothers because of his father's actions. In addition, Joseph would spur hatred through his own interpretations of his dreams. When the opportunity arose, the ten brothers sold him into slavery to get rid of him. Joseph was taken to Egypt where he was sold and became a slave. His owner's wife lied about him maliciously, falsely accusing him of attempted rape and he was imprisoned. He successfully interpreted two prisoners' dreams and ultimately ended up in front of Pharaoh, where he was appointed to be the most powerful appointed official in the world of his day. God decreed both the overt good in the life of Joseph as well as the sins committed against Joseph.

I realize, for some, Sovereignty in all events creates a barrier they cannot traverse. For some, the idea that God decrees good and evil takes God to a place of incomprehensibility.

Let me caution the reader against saying, "My God would never do___," and you fill in the blank with whatever your God will not do. Putting limitations beyond what the Bible does for God's behavior is creating your own God, an idol. If you take this track you are creating your own God after your image. For many, the god they have placed in a nice, neat little box, or the god they have created cannot co-exist with this God who is now so vastly complex. A great deal of current religious thought, even in the church, is centered on human wisdom laced with our democratic and individualistic culture. The simple presentation of Yahweh in scripture is that He is autocratic; He rules by the counsel of His own will and He does not consult the created. God does not think or reason as our present American culture.

The great Calvinistic Baptist preacher Charles Spurgeon made the following point:

> On the other hand, there is no doctrine more hated by worldlings, no truth of which they have made such a football -- as the great, stupendous, but yet most certain doctrine, of the sovereignty of the infinite Jehovah. Men will allow God to be everywhere, except on His throne. They will allow Him to be in His workshop to fashion worlds and make stars. They will allow Him to be in His almonry to dispense His alms and bestow His bounties. They will allow Him to sustain the earth and bear up the pillars thereof, or light the lamps of heaven, or rule the waves of the ever-moving ocean; but when God ascends His throne -- then His creatures gnash their teeth! ... We proclaim an enthroned God, and His right to do as He wills with His own, to dispose of His creatures as He

thinks well, without consulting them in the matter. Then it is, that we are hissed and execrated; and then it is, that men turn a deaf ear to us -- for God on His throne -- is not the God they love. But it is God upon the throne that we love to preach. It is God upon His throne, whom we trust!"[2]

It may grate on our nerves that God is truly the only autonomous, truly free being, because so much of our theology is ego-centric rather than theo-centric. The only way to properly understand the Bible and what God is doing is to realize that God exercises the same authority in the governance of creation as He did in making the creation. These straw-gods we create that are like us, that reason like we humans do and make sense to us, are burned up in the disclosure of Yahweh who is simply different. That God is vastly different than we think, incomprehensible, should not stymie us. Truth does not rise or fall on our comprehension but on its own merit and factuality. Truth is truth not because you believe it is true. The post-modern concept that the veracity of Truth requires common agreement is nonsense. The laws of mathematics and physics do not depend on our agreement for them to be Truth. Biblical Truth must be free from the tyranny of our agreement.

We must always go to Scripture. The bellwether of truth is not our personal reason but God's revealed word. God's word has plenty to say about God and His sovereign authority.

Thus says the LORD, the King of Israel and his Redeemer, the LORD of hosts: "I am the first and I am the last, besides me there is no god. Who is like me? Let him proclaim it. Let him declare and set it before me, since I appointed an ancient people. Let them declare what is to come, and what

---

2   Charles Spurgeon, "Divine Sovereignty," sermon delivered at New Park Street Chapel (1856), found on-line at The New Park Street Pulpit, http://www.spurgeon.org/sermons/0077.htm

will happen. Fear not, nor be afraid; have I not told you from of old and declared it? And you are my witnesses! Is there a God besides me? There is no Rock; I know not any." (Isaiah 44:6-8)* [3]

God decrees. He decreed every aspect of creation, of all that exists ex-nihilo. God decreed man as the apex of creation. He decreed the events in the life of Abraham, Isaac and Jacob. God also decreed the life of Joseph: his suffering and exultation, the salvation of his family.

The decree of God is immutable "…none can stay his hand," All of the events in Joseph's life conformed to divine decree or fiat. We must also conclude that part of the immutable decree of God for Joseph was that he would suffer injustice.

That God would purpose such a thing as injustice to further His own plan for Joseph is a hard truth as we have discussed. It is important for us to realize that what is inconceivable for us in our earthly perspective is not inconceivable to God. We go back to the Bible again for instruction.

For my thoughts are not your thoughts, neither are your ways my ways, declares the LORD For as the heavens are higher than the earth, so are my ways higher than your ways and my thoughts than your thoughts. (Isaiah 55: 8, 9)

That God would and does decree injustice is a hard truth but we cannot shy away from it without doing violence to the Biblical text. The critical piece of it all is to remember that, yes, God did decree injustice but the injustice was not without purpose. We are better served to never isolate suffering from God's intended good purpose whether we grasp the scope of the good or not.

We must not focus solely on an event or events in our lives as if they are a photograph or film frame in a movie; we must see

---

3   See Note marked * at chapter end.

the whole story. Joseph, if he had been stuck in the history of his imprisonment, not seeing the larger context of an audience with Pharaoh and advancement would become a truly tragic figure.

God ordains that Christians will be sinned against. Yet those who sin against us will answer to God for what they do because of the message contained in the book of Revelation and elsewhere. God will judge the world for its actions. Justice delayed will not be justice denied.

Mitchell Chase in his book *Behold our Sovereign God* says,

> The Bible doesn't tell us how God is able to ordain sin and suffering, hold us accountable for real choices, yet not be blamed himself. Nevertheless, we must believe several biblical truths at the same time: (1) God is sovereign over all sin, (2) man is responsible for his own iniquity, and (3) God is just and has authority to judge the wicked, since (4) the wicked sin according to their own evil desires. Don't let certain snares of philosophical logic keep you from embracing all that the Bible teaches about God's sovereignty. His ways are often mysterious, his thoughts are wiser than ours will ever be, his motives are always righteous, and his deeds are never wrong. He is good and does good. ...If the Bible guides believers to hold several truths simultaneously— which may at first seem contradictory— then we must submit our minds to his word and admit the element of mystery. We can't fully articulate how God can be both three distinct yet indivisible persons and one divine being, but we believe in the trinity. We can't fully articulate how Jesus is both fully divine and fully human, but we believe in the incarnation of the Son of God. We can't fully articulate how the sinless Son of God bore the wrath of his Father for the iniquity of the world, but we believe in the propitiatory and substitutionary work of the cross. We believe certain doctrines not because they're always explicable but because they're

biblical. They may provoke questions or stir controversy, but hopefully such doctrines— doctrines— particularly the sovereignty of God— will be an anchor for our souls and a reason for relentless trust in our all-wise God who does all things well.[4]

An anchor. We need an anchor for our souls when the hurricane winds of life, bound up in the evil of others, would knock us off our feet spiritually. Everything that Satan would throw at us has the insidious purpose of causing us to doubt the goodness and love of God. When evil assailed Joseph through the actions of his ten bothers, the malice of his master's wife, and the shallow forgetfulness of the cupbearer, Joseph needed that anchor. We need that same anchor when our life and those around us are seemingly out of control. We need to know God is enthroned on high and is still very much in control of His creation and our lives.

All of the events recorded in Genesis chapters 37-50 were part of a redemptive scenario for Joseph and his family. In other words, injustice, for Joseph, was not the final word. Injustice is never God's end-game.   God's governance of this world also transcends into the next world. That is to say God's will is done ultimately in heaven and Earth. What that means for us is that the work of God in our individual lives, in our families, our communities, our nation, and our world does not stop in this life. What begins here on Earth truly does not end here on Earth. This is where the concept of the final judgment comes into play. Even if injustice runs through the entire course of our present lives, the sure promise that we have is that injustice will not be ignored. God will make all things ultimately right; he will balance the books.

We make this point in the strongest possible terms because

---

4   Mitchell L. Chase, *Behold Our Sovereign God: All Things From Him, Through Him, and To Him* (Houston: Lucid Books, 2012, Kindle Edition)

experience teaches us that not all injustice in life is answered in this life; indeed there is much injustice where there is simply no final accounting in the here and now. Joseph Stalin, through his direct governance, murdered millions of his own countrymen, yet he died in his bed. If we care to look, we can find other examples of the same moral inequity. So we need to know that justice will be done. Injustice and suffering are part of the cosmic parade of history but God will end suffering and bring about justice.

In much of modern western Christianity, there is an almost allergic reaction against the study of theology, hence the rise in non-denominationalism. It seems as if we fear being labeled theologically as ascribing to any particular theological system; we are theologically adverse. This willingness to minimize the study of serious theology does not serve us well. Sure, we can all sit around and sing worship songs and feel good but that good feeling can quickly dissipate when life blows against us as a storm against the wall. This life is deep, complex, and often hard so we need a theology that can sustain our souls. Deep theology is a blessed anchor for us. God's sovereignty, His divine decrees that order our lives, are not our bane, they are our blessing.

> Sin and Suffering Serve the Purposes of God... God rules with purpose. The Bible reveals a sovereign God who rules his world with intent, not randomness. Since God's rule encompasses all creation— good and evil— there is no such thing as a meaningless event. If something appears meaningless, remember we have a limited vantage point...God's purposes are often concealed. Knowing God has purposes for sin and suffering is not the same as knowing the content of those purposes.[5]

The life of Joseph is a microcosm of God's work in the narrative of history.

---

5   Ibid.

NOTES:

* Following are more scriptures on sovereignty and God's predestination. The list is certainly not exhaustive. When I started my Christian journey I was a confirmed Armenian, believing that God saves those who make a choice to turn to Him in saving faith, confessing Christ as Savior and Lord. Frankly, I would get upset with people who took a Calvinistic stance. A careful study of the Westminster Confession (on a dare) and Romans chapter nine changed my perspective. I respect those who hold my previous opinion, and my aim is not to 'convert' (as a good Calvinist, I say that God does the converting) but to explain. I am sensitive to those who have theological or philosophical problems with Calvinism but it is important to me to teach the whole counsel of God as I understand it.

Some Calvinists are insufferable, I am afraid (I have met some). Calvinism is a theological system, a frame of reference and understanding, but to state the obvious, it does not save us from our sins and impart rebirth. Proper Calvinism is always focused on the goodness and glory of God. The triune God is exalted.

Proper Calvinism exalts God as we see in Revelation 4: 8-11:

And the four living creatures, each of them with six wings, are full of eyes all around and within, and day and night they never cease to say, "Holy, holy, holy, is the Lord God Almighty, who was and is and is to come!" And whenever the living creatures give glory and honor and thanks to him who is seated on the throne, who lives forever and ever, the twenty-four elders fall down before him who is seated on the throne and worship him who lives forever and ever. They cast their crowns before the throne, saying "Worthy are you, our Lord and God, to receive glory and honor and power, for you created all things, and by your will they ex-

isted and were created."

Behold, to the LORD your God belong heaven and the heaven of heavens, the earth with all that is in it. (Deuteronomy 10:14)

The LORD kills and brings to life; he brings down to Sheol and raises up. The LORD makes poor and makes rich; he brings low and he exalts. He raises up the poor from the dust; he lifts the needy from the ash heap to make them sit with princes and inherit a seat of honor. For the pillars of the earth are the LORD's, and on them he has set the world. (1 Samuel 2:6-8)

Yours, O LORD, is the greatness and the power and the glory and the victory and the majesty, for all that is in the heavens and in the earth is yours. Yours is the kingdom, O LORD, and you are exalted as head above all. (1 Chronicles 29:11)

Who has measured the waters in the hollow of his hand and marked off the heavens with a span, enclosed the dust of the earth in a measure and weighed the mountains in scales and the hills in a balance? Who has measured the Spirit of the LORD, or what man shows him his counsel? Whom did he consult, and who made him understand? Who taught him the path of justice, and taught him knowledge, and showed him the way of understanding? Behold, the nations are like a drop from a bucket, and are accounted as the dust on the scales; behold, he takes up the coastlands like fine dust. Lebanon would not suffice for fuel, nor are its beasts enough for a burnt offering. All the nations are as nothing before him, they are accounted by him as less than nothing and emptiness. (Isaiah 40:12-17)

At the end of the days I, Nebuchadnezzar, lifted my eyes to heaven, and my reason returned to me, and I blessed the Most High, and praised and honored him who lives forever, for his dominion is an everlasting dominion, and his kingdom endures from generation to generation; all the inhabitants of the earth are accounted as nothing, and he does according to his will among the host of heaven and among the inhabitants of the earth and none can stay his hand or say to him, "What have you done?" (Daniel 4:34-35)

...this Jesus, delivered up according to the definite plan and foreknowledge of God, you crucified and killed by the hands of lawless men. (Acts 2:23)

...for truly in this city there were gathered together against your holy servant Jesus, whom you anointed, both Herod and Pontius Pilate, along with the Gentiles and the peoples of Israel, to do whatever your hand and your plan had predestined to take place. (Acts 4:27, 28)

For those whom he foreknew he also predestined to be conformed to the image of his Son, in order that he might be the firstborn among many brothers. And those whom he predestined he also called, and those whom he called he also justified, and those whom he justified he also glorified. (Romans 8:29, 30)

I am speaking the truth in Christ—I am not lying; my conscience bears me witness in the Holy Spirit— that I have great sorrow and unceasing anguish in my heart. For I could wish that I myself were accursed and cut off from Christ for the sake of my brothers, my kinsmen according to the flesh. They are Israelites, and to them belong the adoption, the glory, the covenants, the giving of the law,

*the worship, and the promises. To them belong the patri-
archs, and from their race, according to the flesh, is the
Christ, who is God over all, blessed forever. Amen. But it
is not as though the word of God has failed. For not all
who are descended from Israel belong to Israel, and not all
are children of Abraham because they are his offspring, but
"Through Isaac shall your offspring be named." This means
that it is not the children of the flesh who are the children
of God, but the children of the promise are counted as offspring. For this is what the promise said: "About this time
next year I will return, and Sarah shall have a son." And
not only so, but also when Rebekah had conceived children
by one man, our forefather Isaac, though they were not yet
born and had done nothing either good or bad—in order
that God's purpose of election might continue, not because
of works but because of him who calls— she was told,
"The older will serve the younger." As it is written, "Jacob I
loved, but Esau I hated." What shall we say then? Is there
injustice on God's part? By no means! For he says to Moses,
"I will have mercy on whom I have mercy, and I will have
compassion on whom I have compassion." So then it depends not on human will or exertion, but on God, who has
mercy. For the Scripture says to Pharaoh, "For this very
purpose I have raised you up, that I might show my power
in you, and that my name might be proclaimed in all the
earth." So then he has mercy on whomever he wills, and he
hardens whomever he wills. You will say to me then, "Why
does he still find fault? For who can resist his will?"0 But
who are you, O man, to answer back to God? Will what
is molded say to its molder, "Why have you made me like
this?" Has the potter no right over the clay, to make out of
the same lump one vessel for honorable use and another
for dishonorable use? What if God, desiring to show his
wrath and to make known his power, has endured with
much patience vessels of wrath prepared for destruction,*

in order to make known the riches of his glory for vessels of mercy, which he has prepared beforehand for glory— even us whom he has called, not from the Jews only but also from the Gentiles? 25 As indeed he says in Hosea, "Those who were not my people I will call 'my people,' and her who was not beloved I will call 'beloved.'" "And in the very place where it was said to them, 'You are not my people,' there they will be called 'sons of the living God.'" And Isaiah cries out concerning Israel: "Though the number of the sons of Israel be as the sand of the sea, only a remnant of them will be saved, for the Lord will carry out his sentence upon the earth fully and without delay." And as Isaiah predicted, "If the Lord of hosts had not left us offspring, we would have been like Sodom and become like Gomorrah." What shall we say, then? That Gentiles who did not pursue righteousness have attained it, that is, a righteousness that is by faith; but that Israel who pursued a law that would lead to righteousness did not succeed in reaching that law. Why? Because they did not pursue it by faith, but as if it were based on works. They have stumbled over the stumbling stone, as it is written, "Behold, I am laying in Zion a stone of stumbling, and a rock of offense; and whoever believes in him will not be put to shame." (Romans 9)

Blessed be the God and Father of our Lord Jesus Christ, who has blessed us in Christ with every spiritual blessing in the heavenly places, even as he chose us in him before the foundation of the world, that we should be holy and blameless before him. In love he predestined us for adoption as sons through Jesus Christ, according to the purpose of his will, to the praise of his glorious grace, with which he has blessed us in the Beloved. (Ephesians 1:3-6)

In him we have obtained an inheritance, having been pre-

destined according to the purpose of him who works all things according to the counsel of his will, (Ephesians 1:11)

CHAPTER SIX

JOSEPH, THE FAVORED SON

Jacob lived in the land of his father's sojournings, in the land of Canaan. These are the generations of Jacob. Joseph, being seventeen years old, was pasturing the flock with his brothers. He was a boy with the sons of Bilhah and Zilpah, his father's wives. And Joseph brought a bad report of them to their father. Now Israel loved Joseph more than any other of his sons, because he was the son of his old age. And he made him a robe of many colors. But when his brothers saw that their father loved him more than all his brothers, they hated him and could not speak peacefully to him. (Genesis 37:1-4)

So we begin, for our purposes, the narrative of Joseph's life. He began, at least in his father's eyes, favored and marked for greatness. If we think back to our experiences at school perhaps, we all can remember an individual or two that just seemed to have it all together. Good looks, perhaps athletic ability, top scholars that just seemed to live in the rarified atmosphere of 4.0 GPA. People, we recall, who seemed to be on the cusp of greatness and should go far. Joseph would have likely fallen into this category if he was our contemporary.

Jacob, Joseph's father, now lives in the land promised to his grandfather, Abraham. He is a wealthy herdsman; he is rich in cattle and possessions and sons. You can say what you like about Jacob, but the fact of the matter is he did not get to the position that he occupied without a lot of hard work. God has blessed him and blessed his efforts.

However there is trouble on the horizon for Jacob and his family. For all of Jacob's ability as a businessman, he did have some serious deficits as a father. This has been a pervasive problem down through history for many accomplished people. For example Henry Ford, as brilliant as he was an inventor and businessman, also made terrible decisions as a parent. Henry Ford's drive for success, his passion for perfection, and his need for control broke his son's health and helped send him to an early grave.

As we mentioned previously, favoritism was a family of origin issue for Jacob. Instead of seeing the potential problems inherent in such action (as he well should have given his history with Esau), he engaged in obvious, naked favoritism of his son, Joseph. We read that because Joseph was a son born in Jacob's old-age, he placed him in an exalted position going so far as to dress him in clothing superior to anything that his other sons had to wear. According to the chronology in Genesis, Jacob was ninety-one years old when Joseph was born, a son born to his beloved Rachel.[1]

Although Joseph is the second youngest son of Jacob, he marked him with privilege unfitting for his rank among the brothers. We read that Jacob presented Joseph with a special garment. There is a difference of translations in various Bible versions as to the particulars of the clothing given to Joseph. For example, the English Standard Version and King James Version detail it as "…a robe of many colors…." Conversely, the Ortho-

---

1 We know that Joseph was thirty-nine when he reunited with Jacob (Genesis 41:46; 45:6)—it was during the ninth year of the fourteen year bumper crop/famine cycle. Jacob was one hundred thirty years old (Genesis 47:9).

dox Jewish Bible, The Young's Literal Translation and the Complete Jewish Bible all explain it as a long-sleeved coat or robe. Maybe if we combine the two thoughts it was multi-colored and long-sleeved. We are admittedly conjecturing here with combining the two concepts. It does seem to be clear it was long sleeved. So why the big deal? Well, think about working under the hood of your car wearing your best long-sleeved shirt and the problem with long sleeves becomes evident. The tunics the other brothers wore were not sleeved, so there were no sleeves to get dirty in animal waste for example. If a farmer had eleven sons who worked for him on the farm and he bought overalls and work boots for ten but an expensive Sunday suit for the eleventh son, the ten would naturally resent the difference in clothing as well as the implication.

The point is, Joseph was marked out with favor that should have been reserved for the oldest son. In 2 Samuel chapter 13, verse 18, we read of the daughter of David, Tamar, who wore a multicolored robe that marked her as a virgin daughter of the king. When she was raped she tore the garment and smeared herself with ashes. Jacob is treating Joseph almost as if he is royalty. Such treatment would not bode well for Joseph's relationship with his other brothers and we need to note that this is not Joseph's fault. For his father to have provided such a costly and ornate garment and Joseph then refuse to wear it, would have been an insult in the highest order.

Jacob's second youngest son was a good boy. Although he was clothed with wealth and dignity beyond his position in the family, he still worked among his brothers as a herdsman. His father did not spare him the necessity and blessing of work and that is a plus mark in the character of Jacob. As Matthew Henry has said in his commentary on Genesis, "Those that are trained up to do nothing are likely to be good for nothing." Joseph worked and he knew how to work. He knew what proper work habits were and when some of his brothers evidentially slacked off, Joseph brought it to his father's attention. To use a phrase of our day,

Joseph became a whistleblower.

There was no maliciousness or ill intent in Joseph's actions. Given his character, as we see it later, there is no reason to think that Joseph was doing anything other than looking out for the best interest of his father. When I was young, I worked in my father's business and I remember my mother saying to me on more than one occasion that she wanted me to keep my eyes and ears open to look out for the interests of my father and mother because the business was all they had. We see the same situation here because all that Jacob has is the herds, flocks, and sons that he has acquired over many years of work. Regardless, Joseph's actions, cobbled together with the ornate dress given him by his father, created problems in Joseph's relationship with his brothers. A simple fact that bears repeating here is that all of these ten men were older than Joseph; they shared the same father but had different mothers. They were half-brothers and so the familial ties were not as strong, certainly in the mind of the ten brothers, as the ties were in the life of Joseph and Benjamin who were born from the same mother.

What we have here with the twelve sons of Jacob is, for all intents and purposes, a blended family.

Doubtless the brothers were very angry with Joseph after his report. We don't know exactly what they were doing that Joseph brought to his father's attention but whatever it was, clearly it was something they should not in keeping with their responsibilities. The report was not good and was very nettlesome as far as the brothers were concerned. We don't like our faults and failures shared and brought to light.

"And this is the judgment: the light has come into the world, and people loved the darkness rather than the light because their works were evil." (John 3:19), so said Jesus to Nicodemus on the night when Nicodemus came to visit him in secrecy. The simple fact of the matter is that when we engage in sinful behavior, when we do those things that we know we ought not to do, we do not want those deeds brought to light. We would far rather they stay in darkness and obscurity.

With our broken nature, when others bring our misdeeds to light or reprove us for our rebellion against God and His word, by nature we do not respond with gratitude or contrition. No, rather our answer to the light of disclosure is often one of pride and anger. The accusatory question is thrown out quickly, "How dare you judge me?" But when we are dealing with what the word of God tells us about our behavior and what is required of us we can rest in the fact that the issue is not our human judgment; rather it is the judgment of God as revealed through His word that comes into play. We admonish with gentleness and humility because, after all, we know our own nature and our own frailties and how easily we fall into temptation ourselves. The brothers of Joseph did not respond with penitence. Joseph's report to his father became another opportunity, another excuse to them for their anger against Joseph. It became another reason for them to wish to do him harm.

In a very real sense, Joseph would be persecuted for doing what was right.

CHAPTER SEVEN

JOSEPH'S DREAMS

Joseph had a dream, and when he told it to his brothers, they hated him all the more. He said to them, "Listen to this dream I had: We were binding sheaves of grain out in the field when suddenly my sheaf rose and stood upright, while your sheaves gathered around mine and bowed down to it." His brothers said to him, "Do you intend to reign over us? Will you actually rule us?" And they hated him all the more because of his dream and what he had said. Then he had another dream, and he told it to his brothers. "Listen," he said, "I had another dream, and this time the sun and moon and eleven stars were bowing down to me." When he told his father as well as his brothers, his father rebuked him and said, "What is this dream you had? Will your mother and I and your brothers actually come and bow down to the ground before you?" His brothers were jealous of him, but his father kept the matter in mind. (Genesis 37: 5-11 NIV)

Here we read of Joseph's two dreams that he shared with his family.

What is readily apparent is that Joseph is a far better prophet at this point, than he is a politician, as Matthew Henry tells us. A dated word that comes to mind to describe Joseph is a blabbermouth. Oh, Joseph was not being malicious; he was not trying deliberately to antagonize his brothers and family. It is just that Joseph, like so many others his age (he is after all, only seventeen years old) did not have the wisdom and discretion to keep his dreams to himself. He did not realize or grasp how his words would sound to others. So what Joseph thought was exciting and fascinating merely added bricks and mortar to the relational wall that already stood between he and his brothers.

That relational wall had started long before. Years before, when Jacob was going back to his homeland after he left his father-in-law, he faced a potential confrontation with his brother, Esau. To say that blood was bad between Jacob and Esau was putting it mildly. When Jacob left his mother and father to go to his mother's family, he left knowing Esau was out for his blood.

So Jacob came home and Esau came to meet him, with four hundred men. Esau is riding with an army. On the morning the two brothers are to meet, the first time they have laid eyes on each other in twenty years, Jacob divided his household into groups to meet Esau. Rachel and her child Joseph were the most removed from possible violence. This was not lost on the other brothers as they all were closer to Esau than the favored wife and child. The message was unmistakable to the older ten brothers: Jacob favored Joseph over them.

The first dream of Joseph was that he and his brothers were working in the field and the sheaf of grain that he had bound stood up of its own accord, upright. Then the sheaves of grain that his brothers had bound, all gathered around the up-right sheaf of Joseph and bowed down as if giving respect and paying homage. Simply said, Joseph's dream enraged the other brothers. The ten brothers took the dream to mean that Joseph would rule over them, totally doing violence to the culture of their family. "Do you intend to reign over us?" the brothers asked incredulously. When we get down to the heart of the matter, truly none of us like to be ruled. Our sin nature lusts for autonomy. The most brazen and prevalent lie of the evil one is that we can live an existence free of the authoritative and loving rule of Yahweh-God without consequence. Satan would gladly see us push for autonomy and then gleefully watch us burn in hell. The course of our lives often boils down to how we deal with proper authority in our lives. There are many people who will gladly accept Jesus as a person with moral authority and wisdom but will in turn balk at the concept that Jesus is far more than a teacher--he is the very son of God who possesses all authority and has all rights of rule. They reject that their lives must be placed under the authority of Jesus, that they must submit to him in faith and enthrone him in their hearts as Lord.

The reader gets the impression that Joseph missed the social clues of his brother's response because he had another dream and proceeded to share this one with family. Joseph recounted how in this second dream the Sun, the Moon and eleven stars bowed down to him. Then Joseph made the tactical mistake of sharing the dream with his father. Jacob responded strongly to this dream and rebuked Joseph soundly. "What is this dream you had? Will your mother and I and your brothers actually come and bow down to the ground before you?" What is interesting to note is that Joseph has a vision for a period of time later in his life when he will indeed rise to great status, but not the time of suffering and trials and growth beforehand.

Jacob made abundantly clear to Joseph that he, Jacob, not Joseph was the patriarch of the family. The patriarch of the family was not elected and he did not serve a limited term of office. By culture and by right Jacob would rule the clan as long as he drew breath and would not cede that authority to anyone. Certainly, he would never abdicate that authority to the second youngest male. Regardless of the exalted position that Joseph held in Jacob's heart, there were, after all, limitations and there was propriety. Joseph, unwittingly, had passed beyond the bounds of propriety. Indeed he had passed the bounds of good common sense when he first shared his dreams with his brothers.

Jacob makes reference in speaking to Joseph about "his mother". The interesting truth is that Rachel by this time was long dead. So perhaps it is a reasonable inference that the mother Jacob is referring to is his other wife Leah. If that be the case, then it might be reasonable to assume that Leah had taken a motherly role towards Joseph and Benjamin. This is a sweet and tender thought that Leah would lovingly take under her wing the children of her sister Rachel. There were honest issues, emotional wounds that Leah bore from her relationship with her sister and her husband Jacob. Perhaps she rose above all of that to be good, gracious, and kind to these two boys who lost their mother. If that is the case, then it speaks well of Leah and her character.

Jacob pondered the dream. After all; he had his own history to draw on with his ruling over the older brother Esau. So perhaps Jacob wondered if Joseph's words were prophetic. As Mary would with Jesus centuries later, Jacob kept all of this in his heart.

Chapter Eight

"Behold this Dreamer Cometh..."

Now his brothers went to pasture their father's flock near Shechem. And Israel said to Joseph, "Are not your brothers pasturing the flock at Shechem? Come, I will send you to them." And he said to him, "Here I am." So he said to him, "Go now, see if it is well with your brothers and with the flock, and bring me word." So he sent him from the Valley of Hebron, and he came to Shechem. And a man found him wandering in the fields. And the man asked him, "What are you seeking?" "I am seeking my brothers," he said. "Tell me, please, where they are pasturing the flock." And the man said, "They have gone away, for I heard them say, 'Let us go to Dothan.'" So Joseph went after his brothers and found them at Dothan. They saw him from afar, and before he came near to them they conspired against him to kill him. They said to one another, "Here comes this dreamer. Come now, let us kill him and throw him into one of the pits. Then we will say that a fierce animal has devoured him, and we will see what will become of his dreams." But when Reuben heard it, he rescued him out of their hands, saying, "Let us not take his life." And Reuben said to them, "Shed no blood; throw him into this pit here in the wilderness, but do not lay a hand on him"—that he might rescue him out of their hand to restore him to his father. So when Joseph came to his brothers, they stripped him of his robe, the robe of many colors that he wore. And they took him and threw him into a pit. The pit was empty; there was no water in it. Then they sat down to eat. And looking up they saw a caravan of Ishmaelites coming from Gilead, with their camels bearing gum, balm, and myrrh, on their way to carry it down to Egypt. Then Judah said to his brothers, "What profit is it if we kill our brother and conceal his blood? Come, let us sell him to the Ishmaelites, and let not our hand be upon him, for he is our brother, our own flesh." And his brothers listened to him. Then Midianite traders passed by. And they drew Joseph up and lifted him out of the pit, and sold him to the Ishmaelites for twenty shekels of silver. They took Joseph to Egypt .When Reuben returned to the pit and saw that Joseph was not in the pit, he tore his clothes and returned to his brothers and said, "The boy is gone, and I, where shall I go?" Then they took Joseph's robe and slaughtered a goat and dipped the robe in the blood. (Genesis 37:12-31)

One April 11, 2009, a dowdy middle-aged woman took her opportunity to sing on the television show, Britain's Got Talent. When she first walked on the stage the response of the judges was underwhelming and the audience expected her performance would be a joke. She was frumpy, seemingly out of place in comparison with the other performers. Then she sang her selection: "I Dreamed a Dream", from the musical *Les Miserables*. The power of her voice simply stunned the judges and audience. Truly the song was most fitting for this unknown singer who had nursed a hunger to sing professionally for years. Susan Boyle dreamed a dream, and in the space of the time it took to sing a song, her life was changed forever.

Joseph dreamed dreams but on this day, Joseph's life changes would be a polar opposite of the life changes for Susan Boyle.

Some life events are so earth-shatteringly altering that we tend to think of our lives as before the event and after the event. There is a line of demarcation, a line that seems to divide our existence into two sections. On this particular morning, Joseph awoke as the favored and somewhat pampered son of a well-to-do family and by nightfall he was a slave. That particular morning, he awoke and his life seemed assured with fortune and blessings on his horizon; that night, doubtless, he wondered just how long he would survive. It was the most stunning of reversals for any person's life imaginable.

It all started out easily and innocently enough. We read that ten of Jacob's other sons had taken their flocks to another location for pasture. Jacob, as any good herdsman or businessman would do, wanted to check on the status of his flocks and his sons and workers. For reasons that are not explained to us, Joseph was not originally sent with them. Evidentially, Jacob had no real concern about sending Joseph to them. Now it is difficult to imagine that Jacob would not have been cognizant of the hostile feelings of the ten oldest brothers toward Joseph. After all, we are told that the brothers could not speak peacefully or civilly to Joseph and it is inconceivable to think that this was not obvious to Jacob. We can only infer that Jacob, either through inattention, or denial did not grasp the level of their animus towards Joseph.

Jacob sends Joseph out to check on his brothers and the flocks. It is almost as if unconsciously Jacob is setting Joseph up for mischief. Of course, as events will show us all of this is under the providential control of God and directed by God for very specific and important reasons. The LORD God is in the details of our lives and God very certainly was involved in Jacob's instructions sending Joseph to travel to Shechem. Joseph was obedient and honored his father, doing what was requested of him.

Joseph and Jacob are engaging in dangerous naïveté; Jo-

seph is going to walk into a trap. Was this part of an elaborate-
ly, well-conceived plan by Joseph's older brothers? Had they
planned to take the sheep some distance away from their father's
camp with hope that Jacob would send Joseph directly into their
hands where they could waylay him privately? The weight of
Scripture as seen in chapter 37 verses 18 through 20 is that, in
fact, their plan was hatched on-the-fly. They see an opportunity to vent their frustration, rage, and hatred and rid themselves of this despised rival for family position and their father's
affections. Their hatred brought them to the point of slaughter.
Hatred full-blown is murderous. "Whosoever hateth his brother
is a murderer: and ye know that no murderer hath eternal life
abiding in him" (1 John 3:15 KJV). Murder is the premier device
of the Evil One. "You are of your father the devil, and your will
is to do your father's desires. He was a murderer from the beginning..." (John 8:44).

Their plan was fairly straightforward and simple. They were
beside a dry well or cistern so they would take him, kill him, and
throw him into the pit. Even at this point, the animosity is staggering. They share a common father; they have known Joseph
his whole life. But the bonds of their affections have been cut
and they are ready to commit a most terrible murder and cover
up.

Given the difficulty of the struggle for existence in the times
of Jacob, it is not too much of a stretch to imagine such ill will and
hatred towards a business rival, or a rival for pasture-land and
watering sites. That is not to excuse it, but that is almost compre-
hensible. Perhaps the spur for action for these brothers was an
underlying fear and sense of dread that what Joseph had foretold
would in fact happen: that they would bow down to Joseph in
recognition of his superior position. Joseph is no business rival,
strictly speaking. He is, if anything, a 17-year-old boy who has
not yet learned when it is smart to keep one's mouth shut. He is a
good boy, but a little lacking in discretion. This anger and hatred
is not so much the result of Joseph's dreams (although that is the

immediate culprit identified) as is Jacob's poor parenting decisions. Jacob thought he could give Joseph preferential treatment
over and above his brothers without any consequences. In part,
perhaps, the brothers hated Joseph because he was essentially a
good young man, and truly better material than they.

There will be a price paid for Jacob's unwise decisions and
Joseph will bear the brunt of it.

Were it not for the intervention of Reuben, conceivably, the
whole affair could have ended right then and there with Joseph's
throat slit, and him lying in a dry well. The Scripture tells us here
that Reuben rescued Joseph by thinking up another plan. His
plan was simply to take Joseph and throw him into the dry well.
Perhaps the other brothers were contemplating leaving Joseph
in the pit to let nature take its course and kill through thirst and
hunger. This plan would be monstrous, completely and immea-
surably cruel in of itself. We're told that Reuben's purpose in doing this was to place Joseph in a position where he could rescue
him later and return Joseph to their father. It was in the plan of
God for Reuben to only save Joseph's life; he would not rescue
Joseph from slavery. Although Reuben did not know it, he was
serving the larger purpose of God.

Joseph arrived at his destination and his brothers attacked
him quickly. We know that his ornate robe, a focus of so much
ill will toward him, was stripped from him. It is as if they are
not only stripping him of this hated clothing but they are also
stripping him of an exalted position. It does not take too much
imagination to see that the robe was ripped off of him abruptly,
even violently, in the process. It would have been an ugly scene
and we can only begin to imagine Joseph's feelings as all of this
happened. When stripped of the robe, Joseph is unceremoni-
ously tossed into the dry well.

Betrayal of this magnitude is as a knife to the heart, as those
who have known great betrayal are all too cognizant of. The act
may take the victim completely off guard, unaware of the dis-
dain, the animus, the hatred directed toward them. Betrayal is

the action of a lover, of family, or a close friend that shatters affections, our assumptions, and even our sense of self-worth. It can shake us to the very core of our being and make us question how we even see reality. It is a wounding to the depths of the soul and heart.

For some reason not explained to us, shortly after Joseph is deposited into the dry well, Reuben left the scene. The Scripture is silent as to why Reuben does this but this facilitates subsequent events. Of course, it was God that directed that he would be out of the way when the next events played out by the brothers, are carried out. God is squarely in the next events. Matthew Henry points out in his commentary that "...God's providence often seems to contradict his purposes even when serving them and working at a distance towards accomplishing them."[1]

The brothers sat down to a meal. As they sat down to eat they saw a caravan passing by, Ishmaelites from Gilead carrying spices to Egypt. It is at this point that Judah thought up a plan. His plan, simply, was to take Joseph, sell him to the merchants, and see the bane of their existence slapped in chains and marched down to a foreign country, never to see him again. So then, in one fell swoop, while making money on the deal, they would be rid of Joseph and not have to do any real dirty work themselves.

Then Judah said to his brothers, "What profit is it if we kill our brother and conceal his blood? Come, let us sell him to the Ishmaelites, and let not our hand be upon him, for he is our brother, our own flesh." And his brothers listened to him. (Genesis 37: 26-27)

The evil that family members do to one another is truly astounding. Police procedure in a murder investigation is to examine initially those in closest relationship to the victim. Statistically speaking, murder victims know their killer all too well.

---

1   Matthew Henry, *Commentary on the Whole Bible* (Peabody, MA: Hendrickson Publishing, 1991), 78. (Original work published 1706)

Judah's words are total hypocrisy. "Let not our hand be upon him..." How can Judah make this statement when their very hands threw him into the pit and then drew him out to betray him into slavery? No, what Judah says here is cruel, cowardly, and callous. The eight other brothers present agree to the plan. They knew they were acting out of hatred and malice in ridding themselves of Joseph but they did not know that God was also in all of these events that served His larger purposes. "Surely the wrath of man shall praise you; the remnant of wrath you will put on like a belt." (Psalms 76:10). Even man's rage is a tool in the hand of Yahweh God. Out of their malice God would bring praise and glory.

Joseph is sold for 20 shekels of silver; this was a common price for a slave. In the code of Hammurabi slaves were sold anywhere from 15 to 30 shekels. After the sale Reuben, returns to find the boy gone. Reuben ripped his clothes in grief and dismay; he is the oldest and considered to be the responsible one. In the mind of his father he will be responsible for Joseph's safety. As we saw, Reuben did want to return the boy to his father. Why? We hope that it was simple human decency and maturity but it also may have been that Reuben wanted to better his relationship with his father due to some previous actions that had created real issues and friction with his father. We don't know the real reason as to why Ruben wanted to return Joseph; we only know that he did want to.

So the brothers have assaulted their sibling. They betrayed him and sold him into slavery and now they have to deal with the issue of how best to cover up their crime. The ten brothers have sense enough to know that if they return to Jacob and try to say that they never saw Joseph, that he simply vanished on the journey, Jacob would be suspicious. So they concoct a scheme, a very devious scheme to lie and cover up their crime.

It all seems to come back to the initial impetus of anger: the ornate or multicolored robe. Their deception is simple; they take the robe, dip it in goat's blood to feign that Joseph had been at-

tacked by some wild beast and killed, the bloodied robe thereby
lending credence to their supposition.

> *"The heart is deceitful above all things, and desperately
> wicked: who can know it?" (Jeremiah 17: 9)*

CHAPTER NINE

JACOB MOURNS

And they sent the robe of many colors and brought it to their father and said, "This we have found; please identify whether it is your son's robe or not." And he identified it and said, "It is my son's robe. A fierce animal has devoured him. Joseph is without doubt torn to pieces." Then Jacob tore his garments and put sackcloth on his loins and mourned for his son many days. All his sons and all his daughters rose up to comfort him, but he refused to be comforted and said, "No, I shall go down to Sheol to my son, mourning." Thus his father wept for him. (Genesis 37:32-35)

In 1993, the story broke that the most famous picture of 'Nessie', the fabled Loch Ness monster was, in fact, a total fabrication by a movie maker who had been embarrassed by a newspaper. 'Nessie' it seems was fabricated out of plastic and a toy submarine in a carefully cropped photograph. What was meant as a joke on the newspaper took on a life of its own with many 'experts' taken in by the ruse. The hoax survived for fifty years. The perpetrators kept the truth secret until, finally, a death-bed confession brought the truth to light. Eventually, almost invariably, the truth comes out.[1]

In the garden, Adam sought to hide his guilt from God, to hide what he had done. There are two common aspects to our fallen nature: sin and seeking to hide that sin. The ten older brothers now will attempt to hide from their father the terrible thing that they have done. We know that they have taken the robe that they tore from Joseph and bloodied it to leave the impression that Joseph was mauled by an animal. Now they bring the bloodied robe to their father feigning innocence and ignorance as to whether this was Joseph's coat or not. It is almost as if, in their hypocrisy, they are trying to persuade Jacob that they had never really paid close attention to the coat at all, that they did not even recognize it when they saw it.

Jacob is shattered to the very core of his soul. He utilized the mourning practices for that culture in tearing his clothes and applying ashes to show his tremendous pain and grief. For many days Jacob mourned the loss of Joseph. His heart was broken. Also it is possible that a tremendous amount of guilt and regret ate at his heart and soul.

Matthew Henry writes:

> Now let those that know the heart of a parent suppose the agonies of poor Jacob, and put their souls into his soul's stead. How strongly does he represent to himself the direful idea of Joseph's misery! Sleeping or waking, he imagines he sees the wild beast setting upon Joseph, thinks he hears his piteous shrieks when the lion roared against him, makes himself tremble and grow chill, many a time, when he fancies how the beast sucked his blood, tore him limb from limb, and left no remains of him, but the coat of many colours, to carry the tidings. And no doubt it added no little to the grief that he had exposed him, by sending him, and sending him all alone, on this

---

1   The Surgeon's Photo http://www.museumofhoaxes.com/hoax/photo_database/image/the_surgeons_photo/

dangerous journey, which proved so fatal to him. This cuts him to the heart, and he is ready to look upon himself as an accessory to the death of his son.[2]

The suffering that Jacob endured was heartbreaking: Joseph was dead, gone. No body to mourn over, no last "I love you"; all that remained was a torn, bloody coat. Jacob was not afforded closure and the pain of that lack would have been intense, almost physical.

Perhaps the closest situation is that of parents whose children have disappeared while traveling. The parents of Natalee Holloway have experienced this unimaginable pain. A child is assumed dead but there is no closure. No body to grieve over and bury. It is a horror, a grief beyond words.

Of course, as we see at the end of the story, the life history for Jacob more resembled that of the parents of Elizabeth Smart. But Jacob did not know then that he would one day hold in his arms his lost son, now the most powerful appointed ruler in the world. Jacob suffered what he knew to be a complete loss for twenty years. While he suffered and wept, his other sons, who knew the truth, kept a conspiracy of silence.

In the beginning, to cover up their crime they acted as if to console their father in his inconsolable loss. Doubtless these men too were all fathers who loved their children. And perhaps it was as they saw the suffering of Jacob that they were able to translate that suffering into terms they could understand. Judah, we know from Genesis chapter 38, would lose two sons to death.

It was in the crucible of watching the pain of their father that the hard soil of the hearts of these ten brothers was broken up. What they had done in a fit of hatred had stolen life, joy, and happiness from their father. These ten men were stupid, shortsighted, jealous fools, but they were not truly monsters! Yes, their action was monstrous in scope, but they were not sociopaths. A sociopath can commit the most heinous crime against another

2   Matthew Henry, 78.

without any guilt or empathy for the victim. What broke their father's heart ultimately led them to a point of facing their guilt and complicity in this crime. They were guilty and they lived with that guilt for twenty years. As we will see later, they knew that they deserved ill for their actions. Through guilt, their hearts were broken.

The mercy of God would not leave these brothers in their guilt and the mercy of God would turn the pain and suffering of Jacob into joy and dancing. The guilt of the brothers and the suffering of Jacob were only a scene in a much larger narrative. It is tempting when we suffer to get so focused on the moment that we cannot grasp or lay hold of any hope for the future. But our God delights in bringing order out of chaos, victory out of the momentary defeat, and joy and peace out of suffering. Make no mistake, the suffering of Jacob lasted for years but God graciously brought it to an end.

CHAPTER TEN

JOSEPH GOES TO EGYPT

Meanwhile the Midianites had sold him in Egypt to Poti-phar, an officer of Pharaoh, the captain of the guard. (Genesis 37:36)

Now Joseph had been brought down to Egypt, and Poti-phar, an officer of Pharaoh, the captain of the guard, an Egyptian, had bought him from the Ishmaelites who had brought him down there. (Genesis 39:1)

Joseph is brought into Egypt where he is sold as a slave. When they sent Joseph to Egypt, did the siblings think Joseph would end up in some large construction project with the likelihood of a short life? We don't know for certain what their expectations were; our text will imply later that they did not think he would last long.

In our modern society we can scarcely grasp the suffering that was bound up in being sold as a slave. But we do have more recent historical accounts from our American history during the slave era that gives some grasp of this difficult fate.

During March of 1859 a massive slave auction took place in

Savannah, Georgia where over four hundred slaves from two plantations were sold to settle an estate. There was no guarantee that slave families would not be sold piecemeal. An article from the New York Tribune provides a haunting account of the events.

> "The negroes were examined with as little consideration as if they had been brutes indeed; the buyers pulling their mouths open to see their teeth, pinching their limbs to find how muscular they were, walking them up and down to detect any signs of lameness, making them stoop and bend in different ways that they might be certain there was no concealed rupture or wound; and in addition to all this treatment, asking them scores of questions relative to their qualifications and accomplishments...'Elisha,' chattel No. 5 in the catalogue, had taken a fancy to a benevolent looking middle-aged gentleman, who was inspecting the stock, and thus used his powers of persuasion to induce the benevolent man to purchase him, with his wife, boy and girl, Molly, Israel and Sevanda, chattels Nos. 6, 7 and 8. The earnestness, with which the poor fellow pressed his suit, knowing, as he did, that perhaps the happiness of his whole life depended on his success, was interesting, and the arguments he used were most pathetic. He made no appeal to the feelings of the buyer; he rested no hope on his charity and kindness, but only strove to show how well worth his dollars were the bone and blood he was entreating him to buy. But the benevolent gentleman found where he could drive a closer bargain, and so bought somebody else... ...The expression on the faces of all who stepped on the block was always the same, and told of more anguish than it is in the power of words to express. Blighted homes, crushed hopes and broken hearts was (sic) the sad story to be read in all the anxious faces. Some of them regarded the sale with perfect indifference, never making a motion save to

turn from one side to the other at the word of the dapper Mr. Bryan, that all the crowd might have a fair view of their proportions, and then, when the sale was accomplished, stepping down from the block without caring to cast even a look at the buyer, who now held all their happiness in his hands. Others, again, strained their eyes with eager glances from one buyer to another as the bidding went on, trying with earnest attention to follow the rapid voice of the auctioneer. Sometimes, two persons only would be bidding for the same chattel, all the others having resigned the contest, and then the poor creature on the block, conceiving an instantaneous preference for one of the buyers over the other, would regard the rivalry with the intensest (sic) interest, the expression of his face changing with every bid, settling into a half smile of joy if the favorite buyer persevered unto the end and secured the property, and settling down into a look of hopeless despair if the other won the victory..."[1]

Joseph was placed on the auction block and he was sold like cattle. How awful; how inhuman and demeaning, being sold like this. We do not know what indignities he suffered during this process. Our slave auction narrative gives us a very basic idea. Did Joseph have any understanding of the Egyptian language at this point? It is not unreasonable to think that at best he may have known only a few basic words or phrases of Egyptian. Odds are there would have been much that he would not have understood. Blessedly, for Joseph, he is bought by an individual to become a slave in this individual's household.

His name is Potiphar. The text tells us that he is an officer of Pharaoh, that he is captain of the guard. It could be that he was charged with Pharaoh's security as in our modern Secret Service. Or perhaps he was in charge of simple security of the palace. He

---

1   "Slave Auction, 1859", *Eye Witness to History*, www.eyewitnessto-history.com (2005).

was a man of influence who had an important position in Egyptian society. God not only sovereignly ruled that Joseph would be sent to Egypt to become a slave, he specifically chose for Joseph the household of Pharaoh's Captain of the Guard. There, for all purposes in the shadow of Pharaoh's household, Joseph would begin his servitude.

CHAPTER ELEVEN

SLAVERY

The LORD was with Joseph, and he became a successful man, and he was in the house of his Egyptian master. His master saw that the LORD was with him and that the LORD caused all that he did to succeed in his hands. So Joseph found favor in his sight and attended him, and he made him overseer of his house and put him in charge of all that he had. From the time that he made him overseer in his house and over all that he had, the LORD blessed the Egyptian's house for Joseph's sake; the blessing of the LORD was on all that he had, in house and field. So he left all that he had in Joseph's charge, and because of him he had no concern about anything but the food he ate. (Genesis 39: 2-6)

God may well be invisible to us in the dark circumstances of life. Darkness, the direct inability to perceive him close by, does not change the fact of his close proximity with us when life is hard. In his book, *Let Me Tell You A Story*, Tony Campolo recounts how when he was a small child living in the city, his mother paid a neighborhood girl to escort Tony to and from school every day. When Tony grew a little older, he convinced his mother to pay him to walk himself back and forth and save the money for the household. And so it happened. Every school day he walked to school and everyday he walked home with no problem. He was a big boy who was independent! Years later, after his mother's death, he learned the truth that she shadowed him so that no harm would come to him, but enough out of sight that he never caught on. He did not know she was there, nor did he see her, but she was present and watching over him.[1]

We read that the LORD was with Joseph. This is a most critical and salient point in the whole narrative before us. Joseph's life circumstances have been completely upended. He has lost his social position and freedom, yet Joseph has not lost his excellent character, his integrity and his work ethic. More importantly, although his circumstances have reversed, God's love and *chesed* [2] favor have not changed. Circumstances do not necessarily show God's favor or disfavor for believers. The tendency is to look at circumstances in the immediate and short term, to see merely what is right in front of us. But a proper perspective on any life is the totality of the life, the full and complete parade of the events from beginning to end that show God's dealings in the life of an individual.

One point that will be made abundantly clear in the life of Joseph is that God is the ruler of circumstances; He is their master and engineers them for his purposes. Our circumstances can change in the blink of an eye. We know this instinctively but we will see very clearly in the life of Joseph how at sunrise on one day, he was a dirty, bedraggled prisoner in an Egyptian jail who

---

1   Tony Campolo, *Let Me Tell You a Story: Life lessons from Unexpected places and Unlikely People* (Nashville: Word Publishing, 2000), 9-10.
2   *Chesed*, a Hebrew word which is translated "loving-kindness or favor." The concept in Scripture is usually applied to God's oversight and favor towards Israel as a nation and individuals. *Chesed* is a concept that is a major factor in the lives of Ruth and Naomi in the book of Ruth. We will see further discussion of *chesed* in a later chapter.

by nightfall would be well-groomed, immaculately clothed and the most powerful appointed official in the entire known world. We must remember these truths that we see here with Joseph.

Circumstances are merely tools in the hand of God to shape our lives. God uses both what we humanly call good circumstances as well as bad circumstances, to develop maturity in our lives, to form and shape us. He is making us into the type of people that He wishes us to be, for His glory. Circumstances are always merely extensions of God's providence and direction. Our circumstances do not exist outside of the providence of God. So when circumstances are not humanly what we would desire, we are still called to trust that we are where we are, in fact, supposed to be. "… give thanks in all circumstances; for this is the will of God in Christ Jesus for you" (1 Thessalonians 5:18). We can only give thanks for all things when we trust that God is in all things. In fact, we can trust that God is in all things, even the mean and difficult circumstances. We can trust Him in these times and rest in His goodness toward us.

Trusting God in hard circumstances is truly the thrust and focus of the latter part of Romans chapter 8:

What then shall we say to these things? If God is for us, who can be against us? He who did not spare his own Son but gave him up for us all, how will he not also with him graciously give us all things? Who shall bring any charge against God's elect? It is God who justifies. Who is to condemn? Christ Jesus is the one who died—more than that, who was raised—who is at the right hand of God, who indeed is interceding for us. Who shall separate us from the love of Christ? Shall tribulation, or distress, or persecution, or famine, or nakedness, or danger, or sword? As it is written, "For your sake we are being killed all the day long; we are regarded as sheep to be slaughtered." No, in all these things we are more than conquerors through him who loved us. For I am sure that neither death nor life, nor

angels nor rulers, nor things present nor things to come,
nor powers, nor height nor depth, nor anything else in all
creation, will be able to separate us from the love of God in
Christ Jesus our Lord. (Romans 8:31-19)

What is the alternative to trusting God in difficult circumstances? The very human tendency, the human response to slavery is slovenly work and a poor work ethic--to do as little as possible to get by and avoid the whip. What we see in the study of Joseph, however, is a completely different approach. It is reasonable to infer that Joseph is simply the best possible slave he can be. He is more disciplined, organized, and efficient than any of the other servants in the household. Joseph is very productive in his work and shows tremendous diligence.

We mentioned earlier that Joseph had not lost his character in becoming a slave. Joseph, when he was in his father's household and when all was going well with him, was diligent and dependable in his work. And we see Joseph, when he is stripped of his position and rights, acting with the same modus operandi: he was diligent and dependable. There is a spiritual principle and rule displayed here. We read, for example, in Paul's letter to the Ephesians in chapter 6 a short discourse on the proper work ethic of slaves who were believers, for their owners. Paul tells the slaves to obey their earthly masters with deep respect and a sincere heart. He equates their deference to their earthly masters to their deference, respect, and love for the Lord Jesus. Paul explains to slaves that the work they do for their master, they are essentially doing for Christ, and their work for their master can honor Christ. Slaves are to maintain a good work ethic, not merely to avoid the slave master's whip but as an act of devotion and service to the Lord. This is exactly the mindset we see displayed by Joseph here in Potiphar's household.

What are the implications in the modern workplace between employers and employees? The most important implication is this: if we wish to advance in position and responsibility we have to be diligent, honest, and work hard. Proverbs tells us "Seest thou a man diligent in his business? He shall stand before Kings and not before mean men" (Proverbs 22:29 KJV). Jesus, in his parable of the talents found in Matthew chapter 25, alludes to the truth of the rewards of diligence. The person who is faithful in a few things will have the opportunity to be faithful over more things. And we see this over the course of time in the life of Joseph.

Also we see in this passage that God blesses the house of Potiphar for Joseph's sake. When we honor God with our lives and live by godly principles even though it may be denied by the ungodly around us, we in fact do provide blessings for their lives. God may well provide blessings for those around us in our immediate sphere of influence, both for our blessing and to magnify his own goodness and character. God favored Joseph's master for Joseph's sake.

CHAPTER TWELVE

INJUSTICE, FALSELY ACCUSED FOR RIGHTEOUSNESS' SAKE PART 1

Now Joseph was handsome in form and appearance. And after a time his master's wife cast her eyes on Joseph and said, "Lie with me." (Genesis 39: 6b-7)

Life, often, this side of heaven, is not fair. Injustice is rampant. Injustice surrounds us. Injustice is a by-product of a fallen world.

At the time of this writing, the verdict in the George Zimmerman-Trayvon Martin trial was just announced with Zimmerman being acquitted. Protests are currently sweeping the nation in response to what is perceived by many as an unjust verdict. Regardless as to how we as individuals may line up on this verdict, what cannot be ignored is that perceived and actual past injustices call this judgment of the courts into question in the minds of many.

The names of injustice are legion. It may be rumors spread around the water-cooler at work or even, regrettably, the church pew. Sometimes injustice comes in the guise of promotion denied for reasons unrelated to job fitness but for, in the mind of the applicant, slight or insignificant factors. Maybe the injustice is bound in government or corporate policy that is unresponsive or uncaring about individual needs and circumstances. Sometimes, injustice is far more cruel, more heinous because it involves an abuse of the legal system. Our narrative with Joseph shows this is not a new problem.

In his book, *An Innocent Man: Murder and Injustice in a Small Town*, John Grisham tells us the story of a man accused and almost executed for a crime he did not commit. Ron Williamson dreamed of playing major league baseball but alcohol and injury curtailed his career in the baseball minor leagues, so he returned to his home in Ada, Oklahoma. Depressed over his failure, Williamson turned increasingly to drink which lead to erratic behavior, making him a community nuisance.

On December 8, 1982, a local waitress was found brutally murdered in her apartment. The police investigation was frankly poor and no immediate arrests were made. However, that would change five years later when Williamson and a friend were arrested for the murder. Ultimately, with questionable evidence, Williamson was placed on death row. Ron Williamson was mentally ill; prison for him was a living hell. His experiences on death-row exacerbated his mental and psychological decline.

After eleven years on death row, Williamson and his friend were exonerated and won a judgment against the city of Ada. As it turned out, another man was convicted of the murder in 2006.

When I first read Grisham's book it left me almost physically ill. Prosecutorial misconduct, playing loose and fast with the facts of the case to achieve a conviction, is a total subversion of the justice system. As much as we might like to think differently these injustices do occur and innocent men and women are sent to jail for crimes they have not committed. Now I am not naïve; I know there are many imprisoned who would quickly maintain their innocence all the while lying through their teeth. But as Grisham's book shows, there are people who were falsely accused and falsely imprisoned. It makes us wonder how many have been unfairly executed over the years. Placing anyone on death row should require incontrovertible evidence.

We as Christians should care deeply about the whole issue of justice versus injustice, for Scripture has much to say on these matters. It is clear that God is vitally concerned that the poor and the sojourners receive fair treatment. We see this in both the Old and the New Testament.

Justice and judgment are inclusive. Justice demanded judgment for the spilling of Abel's blood, for example. Justice is demanded of us by God in the Pentateuch: "You shall not pervert the justice due to the sojourner or to the fatherless, or take a widow's garment in pledge" (Deuteronomy 24:17). The law of gleaning, for example, was designed to help feed the poor and the foreigner.[1] Land property rights were protected from generation to generation. Under the Torah law people had a right to their ancestral property, and if it was sold due to financial reverse, there were legal remedies to redeem said property.

It is clear from Scripture that the reality of some people prospering more than others was acknowledged. Any stigma against wealth was not on the issue of wealth itself. However, if that wealth was gained through oppression and injustice, then it was roundly condemned.

What is clear from even a casual reading of Scripture is that leaders were expected to promote justice. Justice was addressed by the great kings of Israel, by David and Solomon both in the Psalms and the Proverbs. However, in the aftermath of their regency, injustice became more and more an issue in Jewish society.

For example, we read in 1 Kings 21, King Ahab wanted to purchase an adjacent piece of property to his palace and plant a garden. The owner of the property, Naboth, was loath to sell his ancestral land and refused to do so. Naboth was perfectly within his rights to keep his land. Ahab's evil wife had Naboth murdered so that her husband could take the land. For this terrible injus-

---

1   See Leviticus 19:9-10.

tice, God sent the prophet Elijah to King Ahab and pronounced a judgment of death upon him.

As the nation of Israel spiraled downward religiously and ethnically, God called out to the people through His prophets, demanding that they act justly toward others but the call was unheeded. Ultimately, the judgment the prophets warned of transpired. The nation was overrun, Jerusalem was ransacked, and the Temple destroyed. Many of the Jews were forcibly expatriated with their captors and spent seventy years in Babylon.

When Nehemiah was tasked with rebuilding Jerusalem, a problem he encountered was the oppression of the poor remaining in Jerusalem by the wealthy and aristocrats. There were food shortages and the people were reduced to selling their property and even their children to purchase food. For those who borrowed money, they were being charged exorbitant rates, which were in violation of the usury laws in the Torah. Nehemiah put a stop to all of this, demanded justice, the return of land to its proper owners, and the ending of usury. Again, the wealthy were not criticized for their wealth, but they were roundly condemned for gaining further wealth at the expense of justice and in taking advantage of the poorest among them.

Doing justice sits at the very apex of godly ethics in the Old Testament. We read in Micah, "He has told you, O man, what is good; and what does the LORD require of you but to do justice, and to love kindness, and to walk humbly with your God? (Micah 6:8) In the New Testament, Jesus continued the demand for justice. In particular Jesus stood for justice and righteousness (and we should say that justice and righteousness are intertwined once again) when he cleared the money changers out of the Temple. The money changers were extorting their temple clients and Jesus, in so many words, called the extortionists thieves.

In the writings of Paul, in particular in the book of Ephesians, Paul told Christian slave-owners to treat their slaves with dignity and humanity. He reminded the slave-owners (analogous to today's business owners) that they have a master as well, a master that they must answer to for how they treat those who work for them. In the push for social justice today, many forget that there is also a justice responsibility of the slave, or what would today be the employee, to treat their owner properly and work diligently and fairly for their owner. Equity in treatment, fairness in behavior, should go both ways. Christian business owners should be the best employers and Christian employees should be the best employees. That is justice.

We as Christians should strive through God's grace to be the most just of people and to stand for justice in society and in the workplace. We should also strive for justice in the legal system as well. Striving for justice is not job one for us however. First and foremost, we are called to be God's people and to share Jesus, the cross, and the empty tomb. We are not, regardless, to be absent from the battlefront for justice in our society. We also recognize that good Christians disagree as to what justice looks like in all situations. A thorough examination of that point is not the focus of this book. But it is clear from Scripture that we need to have an open heart for others and an open heart to share the love of Christ creatively in the community.[2]

Those who have never been falsely accused cannot begin to appreciate the painful wasp-like sting to the soul of a false accusation. It is bad enough to be falsely accused in the court of public opinion, and as we have seen, infinitely worse to be false accused before the authorities, as in Joseph's case.

It all started with Joseph being an attractive young man. "Now Joseph was handsome in form and appearance," our text tells us. There is nothing wrong with being attractive to the opposite sex; that is part of God's design and attractiveness is a factor in our sexuality. We are created sexual beings. The problem here is not that Joseph is a good-looking young man- the problem is who considers him good-looking. We read that his master's wife cast her eyes on him and propositions him or literally,

---

2   See Endnote *

"... his lord's wife lifteth up her eyes unto Joseph, and saith, `Lie with me'" (YLT).

From the text we know that Joseph has done nothing wrong. There is no evidence that he had flirted with this woman or otherwise invited her intentions. He had not, in the parlance of our day, led her on. Potiphar's wife has been the initiator in all of this. She saw this young man, saw that he was attractive, and began to lust for him.

We learn from this situation that our eyes can betray us. What we see or allow ourselves to see can stir up sin within us. Of course, it is not so much this seeing of something that may become a point of temptation as it is what we do with what we're seeing. Jesus tells us that sin begins in the heart.[3] In other words it is what we do with the stimuli that our sight perceives that can become a problem for us. "For all that is in the world, the lust of the flesh, and the lust of the eyes, and the pride of life, is not of the Father, but is of the world." (1 John 2:16 KJV) We can also look at the history of King David and his consort-turned-wife Bathsheba to see this dynamic at work.

In 2 Samuel chapter 11 where at a time when kings would go to war, David decided to stay in Jerusalem. One evening, when he was walking on his rooftop he happened to see a neighboring woman who was bathing on her rooftop. He saw her in her nude beauty, made inquiries, and had her brought to him so that he might seduce her. David's lustful eyes brought him to a point of sin where he committed adultery and to cover up his adultery, murder. In the Sermon on the Mount, Jesus made the point that if our eye offended us we would be better to gouge it out. Of course, Jesus is using literary exaggeration here to make a point. That point is our eyes can betray us. Our eyes can open a door to sin.

Potiphar's wife evidently made no attempt to modify or restrain her passions. She would have this young man in her bed

---

3   See Endnote **

and so she acted upon her desires and pursued Joseph with abandon; she asks Joseph to become a lover. She is an adulteress. Oh, she may not yet have actually followed through with the act but she is an adulteress nonetheless. She has already committed adultery with him in her heart.

Joseph was at a moral crossroad here. He was a normal sexual being with normal sexual desires. There is no indication he was married and had any opportunity for sexual expression. Joseph had worked hard to get where he was as Potiphar's household administrator and the support of his master's wife could be a real boon for his career. It would have been very easy for Joseph to rationalize any compromise with his moral scruples. Joseph was in a foreign land. He was a slave with no true legal standing or privilege. Who would know? This would be their affair, their secret and unless caught, Joseph would pay no overt price for his illegitimate sexual activity. From a perspective of getting ahead, by any means necessary compromise was, on the face of it, a win-win scenario.

But, as we will see, Joseph would not compromise.

We do not know when and exactly how Joseph was instructed on sexual ethics. The most logical answer is that his father passed down the moral instruction. Joseph understood that there was legitimate sexual expression and then there was illegitimate sexual expression. He understood that God was the one who defined what was legitimate and illegitimate; God is the decider of these issues. Furthermore, he understood that legitimate sexual expression had limitations. Sex with another man's wife was adultery and was not legitimate and hence was not allowed. Of course we know from Scripture that at this point, obviously, Joseph did not have the Law of Moses; that was four centuries in the future.

What we see in the life of Abraham is there were two occasions where, to save his own skin, he lied about the true nature of his relationship with his wife and basically placed her in a position where she could become potentially a sexual partner with another man. This happened with the Pharaoh of Egypt and as well as with King Abimelech. It was clear from the responses of both Pharaoh and Abimelech that Abraham had put them in a very precarious moral position.[4] So we see that in differing cultures, adultery was not allowed.   There is a law written on our hearts.

> *For all who have sinned without the law will also perish without the law, and all who have sinned under the law will be judged by the law. For it is not the hearers of the law who are righteous before God, but the doers of the law who will be justified. For when Gentiles, who do not have the law, by nature do what the law requires, they are a law to themselves, even though they do not have the law. They show that the work of the law is written on their hearts, while their conscience also bears witness, and their conflicting thoughts accuse or even excuse them on that day when, according to my gospel, God judges the secrets of men by Christ Jesus. (Romans 2: 12-16)*

---

*NOTE:

The ways to share are vast. It can be a homeless kitchen, or tutoring at-risk children. It can be adopting a family into the church and providing the skills needed for economic health and good choices. The outreach could be a divorce recovery program, or GriefShare or any number of specialized ministries. Opportunities are literally limitless.

But this is far more than simple social justice programs; any civic group can provide that. We must minister to body all the while recognizing the spiritual component: People need to know the Lord Jesus Christ. Yes, people need to be fed bodily but they need the bread of life. Yes, we want to place our pro-life stance

---

4   See Genesis 12:10-20 and Genesis 20.

money where our mouth is and provide assistance for women who choose life over abortion. It does not one iota of good to say we are pro-life if we are unwilling to step into the messy situations that takes a woman to that place. Ultimately, that mother needs Jesus in her life and to raise that child for the Lord. We are not looking for "do-goodism" here.

**NOTE:

> But Peter said to him, "Explain the parable to us." And he said, "Are you also still without understanding? Do you not see that whatever goes into the mouth passes into the stomach and is expelled? But what comes out of the mouth proceeds from the heart, and this defiles a person. For out of the heart come evil thoughts, murder, adultery, sexual immorality, theft, false witness, slander. These are what defile a person. But to eat with unwashed hands does not defile anyone.'" (Matthew 15:15-20)

CHAPTER THIRTEEN

INJUSTICE, FALSELY ACCUSED FOR RIGHTEOUSNESS' SAKE PART 2

We start here with Joseph's answer to Potiphar's wife's advances:

> But he refused and said to his master's wife, "Behold, because of me my master has no concern about anything in the house, and he has put everything that he has in my charge. He is not greater in this house than I am, nor has he kept back anything from me except you, because you are his wife. How then can I do this great wickedness and sin against God?" And as she spoke to Joseph day after day, he would not listen to her, to lie beside her or to be with her."(Genesis 39: 8-10)

To be less than tactful, Joseph could have slept his way to the top, but he does not take that avenue. He refuses her advances and turns her down cold. Notice what Joseph did not say at this point: he did not tell her that he would risk his own life by doing this. Certainly Joseph knew that if he engaged in this affair and was discovered that he would bear the brunt of his master's rage. What Joseph said is that his master has placed him in a position of trust, that all that Potiphar has was at his disposal, save his wife. However adultery would be, more importantly, a violation of God's law. And that was the final deciding issue for Joseph: he would not commit what he knew was a sin against his God. He went on to say that if he did this, what Joseph calls this great wickedness, which indeed it is, he was committing a sin against God.

Joseph was grateful and loyal to his master and he would not betray his master's trust. He did not want to take advantage of his position at his master's expense. We can infer that Joseph had respect for Potiphar.

The implications here are profound. For example, when Joseph's brothers took him by force and sold him to the slave traders, they thought they were acting strictly against Joseph, and by proxy their father, yet ultimately their sin was against God. We have alluded to the fact before that in the prophets of the Old Testament; God condemns injustice of the Israelites toward their fellow citizens. God considers it not just an affront to the victims, God also considers it an affront and a sin against his own person.

Joseph made it clear to her that he would not sin against his God. As far as Joseph was concerned, this issue was closed and settled, but it was not closed and settled in the mind of Potiphar's wife. She would not take "no" for an answer; she would not relent nor give up. She was at him constantly, seeking to change his mind and lure him into her bed. Matthew Henry made an interesting point:

> The hand of Satan, no doubt, was in it [the temptation to adultery], who, when he found he could not overcome him with troubles and the frowns of the world (for in them he still held fast his integrity), assaulted him with soft and charming pleasures, which have ruined more than the former, and have slain their ten-thousands.[1]

We are not told exactly how long she continued to propo-

---

1   Matthew Henry, 80.

sition Joseph. We are told that Joseph continued to resist her advances. The evil one is not able to create new blessings or pleasures to tempt us. He is, however, a master at using the basic gifts and pleasures that God has given us, twisting and misusing them in an attempt to ruin us spiritually. Sexual expression is a gift from God; the desire for sex is a normal drive, part and parcel of our personhood, our humanity. For our good in Scripture, there are prescribed boundaries and limitations on our sexuality. Satan will take those desires and do his hardest work to eradicate any and all boundaries and limitations. We know this because the temptations to tear down those boundaries are more insistent and demanding in our present culture as it increasingly throws Christian ethics aside. Our current culture and media do not readily lend themselves to any restrictions or boundaries of sexuality.

If we are to live sexually in a manner that is pleasing to God, we need His mercy and strength in our present-day. We need clear teaching today from our churches that defines appropriate sexuality and clear boundaries on our sexuality. Why? Because our current culture is steadily at work to eradicate any boundaries, any limitations on who may have who as a sexual partner or partners. We simply cannot let our present culture decide these matters for us.

What is making this infinitely more difficult in the church today is that there are whole denominations allowing the culture to delineate sexual practices and boundaries. The clear teaching of Scripture is being hastily and thoughtlessly pushed to the side to accommodate a small minority that denies the Lordship of Christ as it pertains to their sexual expression. Certain denominations have become the proverbial chameleon, lying on a piece of Scottish plaid, attempting to match the pattern. The attempt will kill the lizard; it is destroying denominations and laying waste to individual lives.

No, rather than accommodation with the culture, we need a clarion call for a biblical distinctive in our lives.

Honestly, calling the church to live distinctively feels for all the world like swimming upstream. To live Christianly today is a struggle against our own innate sinfulness, against temptation, and against what we see so prevalent around us; but to this we are called. In so far as we live just like everyone around us, if the world at-large sees no difference in our lives due to our faith, then they can logically ask the question, "Why do I need all of this religious business when you are just the same as me? What difference does your faith make?" We in the church are called to live in a counter-cultural manner that arises genuinely from within us. We are not talking about legalisms such as refraining from smoking or drinking; we are talking about a difference in our hearts, in the way we act and react with and to those around us. Are we honest? Are we good employees or employers? Are we willing to sacrifice our time and efforts for others? Can others see the fruit of the Spirit in our lives? Is there a sense of goodness about us?

There was goodness in Joseph's heart and life. Joseph was willing to heed the proper boundaries for sexual behavior and not commit adultery. He was willing to obey God regardless of the consequences. "…Obedience to God is our job. The results of that obedience are God's."[2]

---

2   Elisabeth Elliot, *The Elisabeth Elliot Newsletter* (Ann Arbor, MI: Servant Ministries, Inc., 1999 January/February), 1.

CHAPTER FOURTEEN

A WOMAN SCORNED

But one day, when he went into the house to do his work and none of the men of the house was there in the house, she caught him by his garment, saying, "Lie with me." But he left his garment in her hand and fled and got out of the house. And as soon as she saw that he had left his garment in her hand and had fled out of the house, she called to the men of her household and said to them, "See, he has brought among us a Hebrew to laugh at us. He came in to me to lie with me, and I cried out with a loud voice. And as soon as he heard that I lifted up my voice and cried out, he left his garment beside me and fled and got out of the house." Then she laid up his garment by her until his master came home, and she told him the same story, saying, "The Hebrew servant, whom you have brought among us, came in to me to laugh at me. But as soon as I lifted up my voice and cried, he left his garment beside me and fled out of the house." As soon as his master heard the words that his wife spoke to him, "This is the way your servant treated me," his anger was kindled. And Joseph's master took him and put him into the prison, the place where the king's pris-

oners were confined, and he was there in prison. (Genesis 39: 11-20)

Potiphar's wife's sexual harassment of Joseph continued. There is precious little that Joseph could do, other than turning aside her advances. Could Joseph have gone to his master and unburdened his soul? It is not very likely that telling Potiphar would have been a wise course of action, certainly given the events soon to transpire. This is infinitely worse than any contemporary sexual-harassment in the workplace because Joseph had no legal standing or rights regarding the matter. Frankly, he lived and could die at the pleasure of his master. About the best that Joseph could hope for was for his temptress to finally cast her eyes elsewhere.

Unfortunately her eyes stayed fixed on Joseph.

A day came when Joseph went to the house to work and he was there alone with his master's wife. She propositioned him again, grabbed his clothing and Joseph ran, the clothing pulled from around his body. Joseph ran from her temptation. Was Joseph close to succumbing? We do not know how close he was to giving into temptation but we do know that he'd made the right choice and he took himself out of a position where he could be tempted further.

Being tempted is not a sin. Both Scripture and experience teach us that temptation is a constant in our lives. We are promised very clearly in Paul's writing that God provides help in those times when we are tempted, to help us successfully deal with the temptation.

No temptation has overtaken you that is not common to man. God is faithful, and he will not let you be tempted beyond your ability, but with the temptation he will also provide the way of escape, that you may be able to endure it. (1 Corinthians 10:13)

Sometimes we fall into sin because, to put a fine point on it, we want to. Paul address this issue in Romans:

For we know that the law is spiritual, but I am of the flesh, sold under sin. For I do not understand my own actions. For I do not do what I want, but I do the very thing I hate. Now if I do what I do not want, I agree with the law, that it is good. So now it is no longer I who do it, but sin that dwells within me. For I know that nothing good dwells in me, that is, in my flesh. For I have the desire to do what is right, but not the ability to carry it out. For I do not do the good I want, but the evil I do not want is what I keep on doing. Now if I do what I do not want, it is no longer I who do it, but sin that dwells within me. So I find it to be a law that when I want to do right, evil lies close at hand. For I delight in the law of God, in my inner being, but I see in my members another law waging war against the law of my mind and making me captive to the law of sin that dwells in my members. (Romans 7: 14-23)

In all of this we must apply good, God-given common sense. By that we mean that, yes, God will help us resist temptation but we have responsibility in the whole issue as well. We have to ask ourselves are we placing ourselves in a situation or position where the temptation is stronger? To use a very old example, the alcoholic should stay out of the bar. This writer happens to love cheesecake, however, as a diabetic, the Cheesecake Factory is off-limits.

We need to do as Joseph has done and run from temptation. Solomon, in the book of Proverbs, encourages wise young men to avoid the house of women who would tempt them into sexual sin. Of course, the same applies from the opposite gender's angle.

For the lips of a forbidden woman drip honey, and her speech is smoother than oil, but in the end she is bitter as wormwood, sharp as a two-edged sword. Her feet go down to death; her steps follow the path to Sheol; she does not ponder the path of life; her ways wander, and she does not know it. And now, O sons, listen to me, and do not depart from the words of my mouth. Keep your way far from her, and do not go near the door of her house, (Proverbs 5: 3b-8)

Now that Potiphar's wife is a scorned woman, her attitude and feelings towards Joseph completely reverse. The emotion she would have passed off to Joseph as love now turns to malice and anger. She could not be called a potential lover because the only one she truly loved was herself. Her needs, only, were paramount. If she cannot have him she will now strike out against him, to do him irreparable harm. Joseph could not be in a more precarious situation: he is a foreigner, a slave, and now accused of attempted rape. Her wounded ego will now place Joseph's life in danger at the hands of an enraged master and husband.

Her first action was to accuse Joseph before the other men in the household. She made the issue as public as possible so that her husband cannot but act if he was to save face in his own household. By bringing the issue before the rest of the servants she effectively boxed her husband into a corner where he has no choice but to act against Joseph.

Then she accused Joseph before her husband. She sought to destroy Joseph's reputation labeling him as an attempted rapist and signifying herself as an aggrieved innocent party. This is a terrible injustice against Joseph. Joseph had placed himself at risk to maintain the integrity of his master's household.

The Scriptures tell us that when Potiphar heard her story that his anger burned. Here is an interesting question: why did Potiphar (leaving providence aside for a moment and just conjecturing) not kill Joseph outright? Joseph lived or died at the hands of his master. Why was Joseph not summarily executed? It is conjecture but it very well could be that Potiphar did not entirely believe his wife. As we have said, given the fact that his wife had made this a public issue as far as the household is concerned there was no way he could deal with it privately. The master was effectively hedged in as to his possible courses of action; he could not leave things as they were.

Potiphar has no choice but to punish Joseph in some manner, so the choice is prison and not death. Joseph was sent to the prison where Pharaoh's prisoners are kept. He was truly falsely accused and persecuted for righteousness's sake.

> *...Joseph, who was sold as a slave. His feet were hurt with fetters; his neck was put in a collar of iron; until what he had said came to pass, the word of the LORD tested him. The king sent and released him; the ruler of the peoples set him free; he made him lord of his house and ruler of all his possessions. (Psalms 105:17b-21)*

CHAPTER FIFTEEN

IN THE BELLY OF THE BEAST

But the LORD was with Joseph and showed him steadfast love and gave him favor in the sight of the keeper of the prison. And the keeper of the prison put Joseph in charge of all the prisoners who were in the prison. Whatever was done there, he was the one who did it. The keeper of the prison paid no attention to anything that was in Joseph's charge, because the LORD was with him. And whatever he did, the LORD made it succeed. (Genesis 39: 21-23)

Joseph's former master, Potiphar, was finished showing mercy and kindness to Joseph, but God was not. God was with Joseph still. Although Joseph is in a terrible predicament, he is still squarely in the will of God, right where God wants him to be.

In prison for no other reason than he showed integrity and faithfulness to the laws of his God, he was not abandoned; he is not alone, bereft of comfort and compassion. "The LORD was with Joseph and showed him steadfast love…" we read. Joseph was not alone in that prison, for the LORD, Yahweh-God, the sovereign Creator, was there with him to comfort and to bless him.

At the onset of Joseph's imprisonment, it could be easy to say that his life had gone from bad, but still manageable, to infinitely worse. Joseph has gone from the position of a favored child, to the betrayal of his brothers, to slavery, to false accusations with no recourse, and then to a prison. The point that we see here with Joseph is that in our lives we do not simply flow along and suddenly run headlong into some major trial, which we work our way around or through and then continue to flow down-stream without any further impediment. The metaphor for life is not to float slowly down a river on an inner tube, dodging a stump and then continuing down our way. No a more descrip-tive metaphor of life is white water rafting, constantly dodging rocks and waterfalls. Life is a continuation, a constant process of blessing and trial, blessing through trial, separated perhaps by momentary periods of peace. Even in those moments of peace there are still nettlesome issues to face as there is no such thing as Nirvana in this life; heaven is not here. Heaven is our home but we are not yet home.

As in the life of Joseph, sometimes, frankly often, it seems that our trials and troubles tend to sandbag one on top of anoth-er. By this we mean that we don't exchange one trial for another, often it seems that they begin to pile on. In the book, *Joni and Ken, An Untold Love Story*, Joni Eareckson Tada makes the point that in her life she has exchanged not one trial for another but rather added difficulty upon new difficulty, in the aging process and quadriplegia.[1] First there was the quadriplegia and then the unwelcome intruder of chronic constant pain. As if not enough, she was diagnosed with breast cancer, with surgery and chemo-therapy to follow. The beauty of the story that is told in their book is not the quadriplegia or the chronic pain or the cancer; no, rather the beauty is how all of these things used together have strengthened, deepened, and developed their marriage. It is easy

---

1   Ken Tada, Joni E. Tada, and Larry Libby, *Joni and Ken, An Untold Love Story* (Grand Rapids, MI: Zondervan Publishing, 2013).

to focus on our trials, that seem never-ending and ever increasing. But perhaps a healthier focus is to examine the lives of Joseph, Ken, and Joni and ask, "Where is the Lord with me in this?"

What we would call humanly, bad circumstances, do not mean that God has, in these circumstances, abandoned us, is angry with us, or is necessarily punishing us. There are a whole host of reasons as to why we might be in difficult or bad circumstances, though we have not done wrong to warrant them.

A key point to take away from this passage is that God is always with us in the dark circumstances. When we are in places of darkness where we cannot see His face He is still there. He is our shepherd you know; Jesus calls himself the good Shepherd.

We read in Psalm 23 that when we walk through the valley of the shadow of death, that the Shepherd is with us. He comforts and protects us. In that prison, in that valley of the shadow of death God was there with Joseph protecting him and comforting him. He will do the same for us always. The promise from the writer of Hebrews is that we will never be forsaken or left on our own.[2] Jesus promised His abiding presence with us always in the Great Commission.[3]

God showed Joseph steadfast love, we read. In other translations the phrase, "steadfast love", is translated as "showed him mercy" or "extended kindness". The Hebrew word used here is *chesed*. The translation of the ESV, "steadfast love" captures it well. The idea is of a love that acts with loyalty; the flavor is that of a covenantal love, a pledged love.

Chesed love is a decisional love, a vowed love. *Chesed* is not based on passion or emotion as a criterion. *Chesed* is God saying He is for us and will do us ultimate good as he has promised to do. *Chesed* is stalwart; we can count on God.

Chesed is all throughout the Old Testament in God's covenant relationship with the Jews. *Chesed* love is parental, it cor-

---

2   Hebrews 13: 5, 6
3   Matthew 28:18-20

rects, disciplines and restores as we see for example in Judges. The writing of the Major and Minor Prophets speaks continually of God loving His people with a covenant and offering restoration.

Chesed is always present. This was a lesson that Naomi learned, as we see in the book of Ruth. Naomi felt that God was against her with the loss of her husband and two sons. What she discovers is that God's *chesed* love for her continues with Ruth, in Ruth's loyal love and actions. In a very real sense, Ruth demonstrated *chesed* love for Naomi.

There is still *chesed* love to be shown to Joseph. While in prison Joseph continued to act as he always has, with diligent industry and integrity. This catches the eye of the warden and Joseph is essentially placed in charge of the prison. It is a repeat of the scenario that occurred in the house of Potiphar. In a very real sense Joseph did not allow the actions of others or his circumstances to change who he was at his core. He had a particular work ethic and administrative skills that he would always use wherever he was. It might be easy to think or conjecture that after Joseph landed in prison he may have gone through a period of depression but we do not know that. Certainly if he was depressed due to his circumstances, that would in no way be surprising nor indicative of any spiritual lack. We do know that ultimately, he responded well.

So it begs the question for us: when we are in circumstances that are not of our choosing, where we feel we have been treated unfairly or with injustice, how do we respond? Do we respond with our core integrity or do we get in a snit? Does our character shine or do we sulk? Joseph responds with so much integrity, so much good character, that although he has been kicked completely down the ladder of opportunity, he starts to climb again. The old phrase is very much correct: you can not keep a good man down.

CHAPTER SIXTEEN

TWO CHARGES FOR JOSEPH

Some time after this, the cupbearer of the king of Egypt and his baker committed an offense against their lord the king of Egypt. And Pharaoh was angry with his two officers, the chief cupbearer and the chief baker, and he put them in custody in the house of the captain of the guard, in the prison where Joseph was confined. The captain of the guard appointed Joseph to be with them, and he attended them. They continued for some time in custody. (Genesis 40: 1-4)

Some time after this, ..." Joseph is in prison for an indeterminate time. At some point in his incarceration, events in the royal house lay the groundwork for what will follow in our narrative.

It seems there was a brouhaha involving the cupbearer and the baker that really provoked Pharaoh to a rage. The job of the baker is pretty self-explanatory but the cupbearer should be explained. The cupbearer served the pharaoh his drink; he also tasted the drink to make sure it was not poisoned. The office of cupbearer was a prestigious, important position and one of trust.

After all, the man could literally poison you if he was so inclined.

Not to make light of the two men's predicament, but a favorite cartoon series is Hank Ketcham's *Dennis the Menace*. In one cartoon that seems to highlight Pharaoh's mood, Dennis, his father Henry, and the dog Ruff are sitting in the corner facing the wall being punished. Dennis turns to his dad and says, "Mom's mad, isn't she?" We have no idea what all three did to incur the anger of Dennis's mother against them. Nor do we have any clue as to what the offense was of the cupbearer and the baker, but it was major in the eyes of Pharaoh. After all, he was angry enough to send them to jail. The Egyptian king was an autocratic ruler and could execute justice (as he saw it) quickly without any pesky concerns of the rights of subjects. There was no Magna Carta or Bill of Rights in Egypt. So, for whatever the reason, off to prison they go.

Again it is interesting to note that Pharaoh did not have them summarily executed. The sovereign God is at work and afoot in the anger of this ruler. "The king's heart is a stream of water in the hand of the LORD; He turns it wherever he will" (Proverbs 21:1). God was bringing these two men into the life of Joseph for a very important and specific reason.

The two former members of Pharaoh's staff are placed in Joseph's care by the captain of the guard. Interesting, perhaps, that the captain of the guard has given Joseph this responsibility to care for these two. Potiphar's title was Captain of the Guard. Perhaps it was Potiphar who actually gave charge to Joseph to take care of these two men. Certainly it is an interesting conjecture that Joseph and Potiphar perhaps still had some contact. An even more fascinating question and conjecture is that, had Potiphar understood at this point, that Joseph was falsely accused and improperly imprisoned? Had Potiphar now suspected, or in his own mind confirmed, that his wife was guilty of attempted adultery and perjury? Even if Potiphar had suspected that Joseph's assertions had been right all along given his position he would have been hard-pressed to advocate for Joseph. It is possible that Potiphar's wife had important political connections and or family connections in Pharaoh's household so Potiphar had to tread carefully.

What is important for our story is that Joseph, continuing in his path as an administrator in the prison is given a new task to perform, that of tending to the welfare of these men. For an indeterminate period of time the cupbearer and the Baker are imprisoned under the care of Joseph.

CHAPTER SEVENTEEN

INTERPRETATIONS

And one night they both dreamed—the cupbearer and the baker of the king of Egypt, who were confined in the prison—each his own dream, and each dream with its own interpretation. When Joseph came to them in the morning, he saw that they were troubled. So he asked Pharaoh's officers who were with him in custody in his master's house, "Why are your faces downcast today?" They said to him, "We have had dreams, and there is no one to interpret them." And Joseph said to them, "Do not interpretations belong to God? Please tell them to me." (Genesis 40: 5-8)

In his book, *The Best and the Brightest*, journalist David Halberstam examines how and why the United States became so heavily invested and involved in the Vietnam conflict. It is a fascinating read of hubris and miscalculation. Halberstam shows in great detail how we deliberately set out to misunderstand and misinterpret clear signs that the conflict was unwinnable, silencing and ignoring leaders in government and the military who had grave concerns about the endeavor.

One military man deeply concerned about increased involvement was Army Chief of Staff General Matthew Ridgeway. During the battle between French forces and the Vietminh at Dien Bien Phu in the spring of 1954, there was tremendous pressure domestically in the United States to help the beleaguered French. The French forces, in a show of poor military intelligence and astounding arrogance, had placed themselves in a militarily indefensible position, but many in our government and military wanted to provide military assistance.

General Ridgeway, who had just ended extricating American troops from Korea, was worried about another Far East war. On his own, he commissioned a study of Vietnam, its military challenges, and its infrastructure needs. What Ridgeway learned was that the country would require any where from 500,000 to 1,000,000 men to achieve victory. A conflict in Indochina would be completely different than the Korean conflict or the war in Europe in WWII. In 1965 President Johnson ignored the standing Ridgeway's report. What Ridgeway saw in the crystal ball that was his report in 1954 became a bitter reality in the 1960s because it didn't fit the cold war theory.

We want to know what the future holds; the desire is as old as man. As long as governments have existed there have also been advisors. Egypt was no different. Of course, in those days, advisors were religious leaders and magicians, soothsayers with self-proclaimed, almost supernatural gifts of insight. When Pharaoh had a troubling problem or dream, he could go to these men for enlightenment as, most likely, could Pharaoh's staff.

In these ancient societies dreams could be important, as we see here in the internal evidence of the text in Genesis chapter 40 and in chapter 41 with Pharaoh's dreams. Earlier in Genesis we have the dreams where God communicates with Abimelech and Laban[1]. Later in the book of Daniel there is the dream of Nebuchadnezzar, which in a similar fashion to Joseph, Daniel interprets. Dreams were considered a type of omen that it was

---

1   Genesis 20; 31

wise to understand and if need be, heed.

> *In a dream, in a vision of the night, when deep sleep falls on men, while they slumber on their beds, then he opens the ears of men and terrifies them with warnings.... (Job 33:15-16)*

On the same night, the cupbearer and the baker both have dreams that deeply concerned them. We must not forget the obvious fact that these men are in prison. Their future is uncertain. The cupbearer and the baker have no way of knowing how their situation will end. They do not know if they will be restored to their position, if they will continue to stay in prison, or if they may pay the ultimate price for their misdeeds. Since these two men felt that their dreams were some type of omen, understandably they wanted a correct interpretation of what these dreams would portend. It is very easy for people in a situation such as these two find themselves in that when a dream comes, to interpret it in the darkest possible light. Simply stated, these men are frightened; they are anxious.

The next morning Joseph came to tend to them and he noticed that they were downcast. Joseph was kind and compassionate to these men in showing concern for both their physical and emotional welfare. It is interesting to note that in a place where humanity is often the first casualty, Joseph did not lose his own sense of humanity. Scripture is silent on how Joseph may have suffered and what afflictions he may have borne in prison. Whereas many in prisons are hardened, the thick shells that surround their personhood growing more impenetrable, Joseph still functioned with grace and kindness. Matthew Henry wisely writes,

> Communion in sufferings helps to work compassion towards those that do suffer. Let us learn hence, to concern ourselves in the sorrows and troubles of others, and to enquire into the reason of the sadness of our brethren's

countenances; we should be often considering the tears of the oppressed…It is some relief to those that are in trouble to be taken notice of.[2]

The good work of the gospel is to see faces and not statistics.

Joseph asked the men why they were depressed and they explained they have had dreams that they do not understand. Furthermore, there is no one who can unravel what the dreams mean. They were no longer in Pharaoh's house and had no access to any of the wise men. Again, they are engaging in a human tendency towards fear of the unknown.

God had providentially caused these two men to dream and He clouded their dreams meaning. Joseph asks them rhetorically "Do not interpretations belong to God?" The Collect in the Anglican Book of Common Prayer for Holy Communion tells us, "Almighty God, unto whom all hearts are open, all desires known and from whom no secrets are hid…"[3]

The sovereign God is omniscient. He knows the hearts and minds of all people. God sees to it that His purposes and His plans come to fruition.

> *Remember the former things of old; for I am God, and there is no other; I am God, and there is none like me, declaring the end from the beginning and from ancient times things not yet done, saying, "My counsel shall stand, and I will accomplish all my purpose." (Isaiah 46:9, 10)*

God, in His sovereignty, sent these two men dreams with intent, purpose, and a clear message that He would reveal to his servant, Joseph. Joseph, by making his declaration that the interpretation of dreams belonged to God, essentially gave God all the glory and praise for His being God, Creator, and sustainer. All is from God and all belongs to God and all works ultimately

---

2   Matthew Henry, 81.

3   *Book of Common Prayer* (Greenwich, Connecticut: Seabury Press, 1928), 67.

to God's glory. Joseph did not seek to take any glory, any credit whatsoever, for what God was going to do for these two men. This is the very heart of reformed theology and thought: all glory to God.

God will make the matter plain.

CHAPTER EIGHTEEN

DREAMS

So the chief cupbearer told his dream to Joseph and said to him, "In my dream there was a vine before me, and on the vine there were three branches. As soon as it budded, its blossoms shot forth, and the clusters ripened into grapes. Pharaoh's cup was in my hand, and I took the grapes and pressed them into Pharaoh's cup and placed the cup in Pharaoh's hand." Then Joseph said to him, "This is its interpretation: the three branches are three days. In three days Pharaoh will lift up your head and restore you to your office, and you shall place Pharaoh's cup in his hand as formerly, when you were his cupbearer. Only remember me, when it is well with you, and please do me the kindness to mention me to Pharaoh, and so get me out of this house. For I was indeed stolen out of the land of the Hebrews, and here also I have done nothing that they should put me into the pit. When the chief baker saw that the interpretation was favorable, he said to Joseph, "I also had a dream: there were three cake baskets on my head, and in the uppermost basket there were all sorts of baked food for Pharaoh, but the birds were eating it out of the basket on my head." And

Joseph answered and said, "This is its interpretation: the
three baskets are three days. In three days Pharaoh will lift
up your head—from you!—and hang you on a tree. And
the birds will eat the flesh from you." On the third day,
which was Pharaoh's birthday, he made a feast for all his
servants and lifted up the head of the chief cupbearer and
the head of the chief baker among his servants. He restored
the chief cupbearer to his position, and he placed the cup
in Pharaoh's hand. But he hanged the chief baker, as Joseph
had interpreted to them. Yet the chief cupbearer did not
remember Joseph, but forgot him. (Genesis 40: 9-23)

Notice that Joseph was able to determine the future of these two men but for all of Joseph's stellar dreams of his youth, he cannot now see his own future with clarity. Years have passed and the props have been knocked out from under Joseph's life more than once. Events would seem to call into question any sense of rectitude about a great future for this jailed Hebrew man. Indeed the text makes clear that the primary order of business for Joseph is to get out of prison.

Getting back on point, what about the future of these two dreamers? Well, the interpretations and outcomes were vastly different.

The cupbearer shared his dream first. He saw a vine with three branches that produce grapes in short order. The cupbearer presses the grapes and gives the cup with the freshly squeezed wine to Pharaoh. Joseph declared this a positive, good prophecy signifying that in three days the cupbearer will be restored to his former position, back in the good graces of his liege. In the telling Joseph asked the cupbearer to intercede on Joseph's behalf. Joseph is, in a sense, defending himself.

Excited at the good news of his cell-mate, the baker shares his dream that he had three cake baskets on his head, the topmost basket containing food that the birds were eating.

Unfortunately for the baker, his dream did not bode well. In fact, it foretold of execution and not exaltation: the baker will be hanged in three days. One person will be restored, the other punished with death.

In three days Joseph's interpretation holds true. Doubtless Joseph hoped that his case would receive quick attention. However we read that the cupbearer forgot Joseph. Joseph's life is a mosaic of people letting Joseph down: his brothers, Potiphar and now the cupbearer. But Joseph is not embittered by all of these failures by those around him on his behalf. Perhaps he has a correct understanding of the true state of man. "We cannot expect too little from man nor too much from God."[1]

---

1   Matthew Henry,

CHAPTER NINETEEN

TWO YEARS

Yet the chief cupbearer did not remember Joseph, but for-got him. After two whole years, Pharaoh dreamed that he was standing by the Nile," (Genesis 40:23- 41:1)

For from him and through him and to him are all things. To him be glory forever. Amen. (Romans 11:36)

For us sitting where we do from the vantage point of four millennia after the fact, waiting two additional years as Joseph did for release can seem a small matter. God forgive us if we think so. Joseph, after languishing in prison for an already indeterminate period of time, now waits… again. There is no evidence to show that Joseph thought he would ever be free.

There is so much about Joseph that we simply do not know; the curtain has not been pulled back. We do not know, for example, what the heart of Joseph was in this time. Certainly we know it was a time of further testing, these two years. As we have said, Joseph had no clue as to whether he would ever get out of jail and see the light of day as a free man again. We simply do not know how he dealt with this on a spiritual and emotional level. He was human and doubtless he struggled with his emotions. Was Joseph ever depressed? Did he, in the midst of the realization that he simply had been forgotten and marginalized, question God? He had seen God's favor and mercy in dark hours, even in what is commonly called a reversal of fortune. Was God no longer there?

We do not have the same advantage of self-expression with Joseph that we have with King David. In contrast, King David seems to have told us virtually everything that was on his heart and mind. Through the blessing of the Psalms, the heart and the emotions of David are all an open book. But not so with Joseph: he is at least at this point, a cipher. The curtain into the emotions and heart of Joseph are fully in place and why that is we simply don't know. It would not be surprising-indeed we would think him all the more real and believable-if Joseph had his dark night of the soul.

We do know that God had His purposes in Joseph's continued incarceration and that those purposes were for Joseph's good. God's economy does not waste time. We can surmise that God yet had spiritual work to do in Joseph, that there was a needed additional period of seasoning.

Many of God's people, over the centuries, have spent time in jail. The world does not approve of counter-cultural movements and tends to jail its members. Christians, historically, are counter-cultural. Although in recent centuries in Europe and the United States the culture was somewhat Judeo-Christian, this has changed. We Christians (at least the more orthodox socially/ theologically conservative) are increasingly considered counter-cultural.

Jail is not wasted for Christians. Paul's letters, roughly half of them, were prison letters. John Bunyan wrote Pilgrim's Progress, a book second only to the Bible in readership and printing, while imprisoned for preaching. Confinement can be a tool to sharpen our focus and deepen our thoughts; Dr. Martin Luther King's *Letters from the Birmingham Jail* brought King's perspectives into clarity.[1] Joseph's additional confinement was not a cruel mistake from God; spiritual and maturational fruit grew in Pharaoh's prison.

Is there an answer as to why Joseph languished in prison for two more years? Ostensibly, it seems to come down to a scatter-brained cupbearer, so excited by his restored good fortune that he forgot to extend good fortune to another. Even though the cupbearer failed to act kindly and proactively in the short-term, his knowledge of Joseph and Joseph's gift is crucial to our story and history. The cupbearer will make this right. The failure to remember, the failure to act, was God's purpose at work. God is involved in all things, and was involved even this omission. "For from him…are all things."

But, we ask, why wait? The concept of Occam's razor is the best, non- conjecture solution for the why. What is Occam's razor?

The dictionary defines it (or the law of parsimony) as "The principle in philosophy and science that assumptions introduced to explain a thing must not be multiplied beyond necessity, and hence the simplest of several hypotheses is always the best in accounting for unexplained facts."[2]

The concept of Occam's razor is the most observable solution for why Joseph sat in prison two years after the cupbearer was restored. The obvious truth is that Pharaoh had not yet dreamed his two inscrutable dreams. Two dreams that needed divine interpretation from a God-illuminated diviner.

Timing—everything comes down to timing. That is not to say, as we have supposed, that God did not also have other purposes. We do know there was a time component and Pharaoh had to dream. So often, our frustration on the timing of God stems from the simple fact that we cannot see in our humanness,

1   Martin Luther King, Jr., *Letters from the Birmingham Jail*, Final Arbiter Amazon Digital Services (2011).
2   *Webster's College Dictionary* (New York: Random House, Inc. 1991, 1997, 2005, 2010)

what He sees in His divinity. Although we know that God will bring us home to heaven, we cannot see the intermediate time for our individual lives

In that awesome passage found in Hebrews chapter 11-the Hall of Faith it is sometimes called-we see clearly that not all faith stories end on what we would humanly call, a high note. We see some as Joseph, who suffered great trial and tribulation in this life, move onto great heights of success and achievement; they are victorious in the here and now. But others, we see, have a far different end in this life. What is important to note is that when we say "end" we're talking of this life and we cannot make that point clearly enough. Not all victory is here; not all of the questions, all the "why" are answered. Sometimes victory takes the slipping of this mortal skin for the taking on of the new, eternal dwelling, or what Paul calls so aptly in Corinthians, "this tent...". Sometimes victory comes not now as with many Christians: rather the victory comes in the hereafter.

Consider if you will the plight of Christians in North Korea, or Africa, or parts of the Middle East. Every day, in these various regions of the world, Christian people, those who love Jesus and seek to serve him and walk faithfully with him, are suffering economic and social injustice. Some are imprisoned and others slain for Christ, sheep for the slaughter. The Nicene Creed tells us that at the end of the age, Christ shall come again in glory to judge the living and the dead and his kingdom shall have no end. There are countless Christians who have lived on this globe that will look for that day of victory and vindication. They look for that far horizon, for the victory and vindication that has not happened here.

We are tempted perhaps to come to the life of Joseph for answers for our own individual lives. We can apply the principles of his life (obedience in affliction; making God first in all of life) but we cannot necessarily find specifics that will always apply to our lives. Joseph was a worldly success, but we may not be. Faith is applying the principle truth, God is with us and for us as he was for Joseph, to our specific circumstances. God's providence determines the particular outcome for each of us and we cannot over-generalize or demand that our life and circumstances match that of Joseph. Wise faith leads us to trust God, the triune God, Father, Son and Holy Spirit for our lives. Faith leads us to leave the results up to God.

Joseph had no choice, really (and neither do we in the final analysis) but to leave those results up to the one who gave up for us his only beloved son. We can scarcely imagine what Joseph endured spiritually and emotionally for these two additional years in prison. God was still working toward the time when Pharaoh would have his dreams, the interpretation of these dreams, opening the door for opportunity for Joseph. The crucial timing worked to take this displaced young Hebrew, a prisoner, to a position as the second most powerful man in the known world in his day.

If Joseph had come to the attention of Pharaoh two years prior, he would've merely been, if anything, a miniscule footnote in history. There is every reason to suppose that had Joseph been released after the cupbearer was restored in his office, Joseph would have then fled the country. It was because of the divine timing of God that Joseph was able to come to Pharaoh and utilize the divine gift to interpret Pharaoh's dream and initiate the process that would save many people. The glory belongs to God.

David Kingdon writes, "Though Joseph did not know it then [in prison], the way to his place at Pharaoh's side lay from Potiphar's house through Pharaoh's prison."[3]

---

3   David Kingdon, *Mysterious Ways: The Providence of God in the Life of Joseph* (Carlisle, PA: The Banner of Truth Trust, 2004), 20.

CHAPTER TWENTY

PHARAOH DREAMS

...Pharaoh dreamed that he was standing by the Nile, and behold, there came up out of the Nile seven cows attractive and plump, and they fed in the reed grass. And behold, seven other cows, ugly and thin, came up out of the Nile after them, and stood by the other cows on the bank of the Nile. And the ugly, thin cows ate up the seven attractive, plump cows. And Pharaoh awoke. And he fell asleep and dreamed a second time. And behold, seven ears of grain, plump and good, were growing on one stalk. And behold, after them sprouted seven ears, thin and blighted by the east wind. And the thin ears swallowed up the seven plump, full ears. And Pharaoh awoke, and behold, it was a dream. So in the morning his spirit was troubled, and he sent and called for all the magicians of Egypt and all its wise men. Pharaoh told them his dreams, but there was none who could interpret them to Pharaoh. (Genesis 41: 1-8)

The other night, Anna and I decided to watch an episode from Masterpiece Mystery (this writer loves British mysteries) and to do so required us to stream it live from a laptop. It seems as if we have a computer cable for every occasion; determining which was the correct cable to use, and where to place it was the problem at hand. Finally, in seeming desperation, we went to the owner's manual. Where do we go when we are perplexed and need an answer?

This somewhat encapsulates the problem and the issue that we're going to find in our text here in the beginning of Genesis chapter 41. As we have seen previously, dreams were considered a type of omen, a foretelling, or what could be construed as a warning to prepare for bad events. The King of Egypt, Pharaoh, in one night has two dreams that he cannot recall the next morning.

Before we proceed, we will attempt to identify which Pharaoh we are discussing here. Depending on whose research we buy into, the time period for Joseph can range over two to three centuries. However, for our purposes, based on biblical timelines as well as other historical documents, we will place Joseph's first interaction with Pharaoh in the Egyptian Middle Kingdom, the 12th Dynasty. It seems that Joseph actually held a high position under two different Pharaohs: Senusret II (or Sesostris) and then Senusret (Sesostris) III.[1]

The first dream has Pharaoh standing by the Nile River. The importance of the Nile River to Egypt can not be overstated. It was a source of life-giving water and food, as well as a transportation and commerce highway. In a very real sense, the Nile River symbolized the future for Egypt because without the Nile River there would be no Egypt. In the dream there comes up out of the Nile seven well-nourished, healthy-looking cows. These good cows begin to feed along the river. So far, so good.

Then, up out of the Nile River come seven emaciated, unhealthy-looking cows. These newly arrived cows go stand by the seven healthy-looking cows and nightmarishly eat them. It is at this point that Pharaoh awakens from his nightmare.

---

1   See Endnote *

Pharaoh goes back to sleep and he dreams a second time. In this dream he sees a stalk with seven ears of grain that are healthy and mature and then there grows seven ears of grain that are stunted, blighted by the wind. The stunted ugly ears of grain devour the healthy ones. Pharaoh wakes a second time.

We read that in the morning, Pharaoh was troubled by these two dreams; he wanted to understand if there is any significance or importance so that he can act accordingly. Remembering back earlier in our story when the cupbearer and the Baker had their dreams, they were distraught because they had no one to interpret their dreams, or so they thought. Pharaoh did not have that problem. Pharaoh had a wealth of magicians and wise men that he could call upon to help him discern the meaning of his dreams. These were literate men, educated in the various religions, cults, and worldly affairs. So Pharaoh called his magicians and wise men, his advisers, all together and explained his dream, but no one can explain it. Every one of these men that assisted Pharaoh when he is uncertain as to a decision or course of action, they are all puzzled. "…in an abundance of counselors there is safety." (Proverbs 11:14) is a useful rule of thumb but in this case, the multitude is unhelpful.

Without a doubt, Pharaoh was probably unhappy at this point and getting unhappier by the moment. What good is an advisor if they cannot advise you at a time when you need them most? Experience has already shown us that it is not a good thing when Pharaoh gets frustrated and upset.

So what do we take away from this? Well, going back to the example of hooking the laptop up to the television, going to the manual written by the one who has produced the product is an intelligent choice. Our television is a Vizio and the best move is to go to the manual written for our television and not a manual written, for say, a Sony.

It seems so often that when we are perplexed with an issue or problem that we turn everywhere else except to the one who made us. Some people today question the wisdom of going to a book written between 20 to 35 centuries ago. Why would we, in a modern, complex industrial society, go to a book written by people living in the Bronze Age? Now we can get all fussy over the question but it is a good question. Time and space do not permit a complete, full answer to this question. This question is not our focus here. Consider this however: people for all of our technology, in our core selves have not changed. We still struggle with the same interpersonal issues today as people did when the Bible was written. Apart from Christ we are all still dead in our trespasses and sins. We still need a Savior.

We go to the Bible to meet the God of the universe. We go to the creator who formed all that we perceive with our five senses. We go to the Bible to have a relationship with the triune God. The Scriptures is the operations manual written by our maker and is vital to us. We go to the Bible because it is there that we learn that the fear of the Lord is the beginning of wisdom as Proverbs tells us. By the word "fear" we're not referring to craven or abject terror, it is deep reverence and respect. Biblical fear brings us to a place where we respect and honor God; we seek His will and His direction for our lives.

All of the wise men and magicians in Pharaoh's court were bringing to him owner's manuals from the wrong producer. Admittedly our example falls short because we're not looking at a marketplace of theology and ideas. As Joseph we will be coming from a perspective that there is one true God, the God Yahweh. The answer lay with the true maker of heaven and earth, not an idol made of stone by the created.

NOTE*:

This is how one scholar arrived at a date which seems reasonable but there is not universal agreement on the dating of Joseph:

"The Bible...provides us with some very specific chronological data regarding these events. 1 Kings 6:1, a pivotal reference for all Old Testament chronology, dates the Exodus 480 years before the fourth year of Solomon, accepted by virtually all scholars as 966 BC. This places the Exodus in ca. 1446 BC; a date which agrees with the so-called Early Date for the Exodus.

Next, Exodus 12:40 states that Jacob came to dwell in Egypt 430 years before the Exodus. Thus he came to Egypt in ca. 1876 BC. These Biblical references clearly show that Joseph ought to be dated in the Middle Kingdom... Thus, relying on the Biblical chronology and the historical material, we will place Joseph in the Middle Kingdom Period, under two great rulers, Sesostris II (1897–1878 BC) and Sesostris III (1878–1843 BC)."

Above quoted from C.F. Aling, *Bible and Spade Magazine,* (Summer, 2000), found at http://www.biblearchaeology.org/bookstore/category.aspx?id=5.

CHAPTER TWENTY-ONE

THE CUPBEARER COMES THROUGH

Then the chief cupbearer said to Pharaoh, "I remember my offenses today. When Pharaoh was angry with his servants and put me and the chief baker in custody in the house of the captain of the guard, we dreamed on the same night, he and I, each having a dream with its own interpretation. A young Hebrew was there with us, a servant of the captain of the guard. When we told him, he interpreted our dreams to us, giving an interpretation to each man according to his dream. And as he interpreted to us, so it came about. I was restored to my office, and the baker was hanged." Then Pharaoh sent and called Joseph, and they quickly brought him out of the pit. And when he had shaved himself and changed his clothes, he came in before Pharaoh. And Pharaoh said to Joseph, "I have had a dream, and there is no one who can interpret it. I have heard it said of you that when you hear a dream you can interpret it." Joseph answered Pharaoh, "It is not in me; God will give Pharaoh a favorable answer." Then Pharaoh said to Joseph, "Behold, in my dream I was standing on the banks of the Nile. Seven cows, plump and attractive, came up out of the Nile and

fed in the reed grass. Seven other cows came up after them,
poor and very ugly and thin, such as I had never seen in all
the land of Egypt. And the thin, ugly cows ate up the first
seven plump cows, but when they had eaten them no one
would have known that they had eaten them, for they were
still as ugly as at the beginning. Then I awoke. I also saw in
my dream seven ears growing on one stalk, full and good.
Seven ears, withered, thin, and blighted by the east wind,
sprouted after them, and the thin ears swallowed up the
seven good ears. And I told it to the magicians, but there
was no one who could explain it to me." (Genesis 41: 9-24)

Now God's sovereign plan and divine will come fully into focus. The two years are finished and Pharaoh has dreamed
his inscrutable dreams.

It is not hard to imagine that the anxiety felt by Pharaoh was
shared by all of those around him, his Royal Court, servants, and
advisors. Although they as well as Pharaoh knew the dreams were
some type of omen, it had to trouble them because their futures
were at stake as well. In other words, they had a vested interest in
doing all they could to assist in unraveling this conundrum. This
was no time for court intrigues or petty disagreements; everyone
was working to come up with a solution.

At some point in this process, our friend, the cupbearer,
learned of the dreams. Now, having felt the full force of Pharaoh's
displeasure previously, the cupbearer was bound to do everything he could as well to assist his master. Everybody was rack-
ing their brains and then suddenly, the cupbearer remembered.
Now, after two full years, the cupbearer thought about Joseph
and Joseph's gift of interpreting dreams.

This was not without risk to the cupbearer. What if Joseph,
after two years was in no mental state to do anything? It could
have been potentially disastrous for the cupbearer to have Joseph
brought there if Joseph could not come through at this time. We
know at this point, based upon the Scripture, that the cupbearer

must have felt remorse because he had not done as requested by Joseph. In spite of all of that, the cupbearer proceeded to do his best to make the matter right and now to come through for Joseph.

So it is now that the cupbearer shared with Pharaoh his experience with Joseph. Now Joseph was summoned to the presence of Pharaoh. We may wonder if the bearer of news of Joseph's audience was Potiphar himself.

As is the custom of Egyptian men, Joseph shaved himself. The Egyptian men shaved their bodies, not just their beards. He changed clothes, doubtless, to make himself as presentable as possible.

So now, Joseph, thirteen years a slave and then a prisoner, stood before the most powerful man of his day. Pharaoh told Joseph that he has had a dream no one can interpret and he has heard that Joseph can explain the meaning of dreams. There is no time for equivocation, no time to dance around the issue, because now the pressure is on and Joseph must produce and quickly at that. What Joseph says is truly astounding when we consider it. He testified as to the omniscience of God as opposed to his own inability.

Pharaoh wanted answers regarding a dream that no one else could give him. "It is not in me; God will give Pharaoh a favorable answer." What Joseph did not say is astounding: Joseph did not seek to enlarge himself or increase his own personal statute or wisdom in the eyes of Pharaoh. Joseph did not point to himself; he did not claim to be the answer. Rather Joseph said that the true answer came from God. One can only imagine that in the court of Pharaoh, there was a constant pushing and shoving, a jockeying for position of authority and influence of Pharaoh. It would be the concept of putting your best foot forward multiplied by many times. This is not what Joseph did and it is remarkable; he gave all honor to Yahweh-God.

The answer does not rely in us. The only true answer for all of life's perplexities, for all of life's troubles, for all of life's needs, resides in the hands of He who created all that exists. All, the totality of everything, belongs to God.

This is exactly the point that Joseph made to Pharaoh: Pharaoh's answer lay in the hands of God. That is it, there is no need to look any further or go any where else. The fanciful god's of stone held no solutions for Pharaoh. The gods we create of money and political or social power ultimately hold no eternal solutions for us either.

So although we do not know the heart of Joseph during these difficult days that he endured with any certainty, we can reasonably infer that Joseph trusted in the creator God as his ultimate source of deliverance and hope. Joseph suffered greatly at the hands of others, but Joseph could also see the hand of God in his suffering. Joseph did not allow his trials to dictate his relationship with God; he trusted when the face of God was obscured.

CHAPTER TWENTY-TWO

INTERVIEW

Then Joseph said to Pharaoh, "The dreams of Pharaoh are one; God has revealed to Pharaoh what he is about to do. The seven good cows are seven years, and the seven good ears are seven years; the dreams are one. The seven lean and ugly cows that came up after them are seven years, and the seven empty ears blighted by the east wind are also seven years of famine. It is as I told Pharaoh; God has shown to Pharaoh what he is about to do. There will come seven years of great plenty throughout all the land of Egypt, but after them there will arise seven years of famine, and all the plenty will be forgotten in the land of Egypt. The famine will consume the land, and the plenty will be unknown in the land by reason of the famine that will follow, for it will be very severe. And the doubling of Pharaoh's dream means that the thing is fixed by God, and God will shortly bring it about. Now therefore let Pharaoh select a discerning and wise man, and set him over the land of Egypt. Let Pharaoh proceed to appoint overseers over the land and take one-fifth of the produce of the land of Egypt during the seven plentiful years. And let them gather all the food of these

good years that are coming and store up grain under the
authority of Pharaoh for food in the cities, and let them
keep it. That food shall be a reserve for the land against
the seven years of famine that are to occur in the land of
Egypt, so that the land may not perish through the famine."
(Genesis 41: 25-36)

The court of Pharaoh, the royal magicians and advisors, all heard the same information that Pharaoh recounted to Joseph, but Joseph alone explained the dream.

Once again God worked for the good of Joseph. As he was with Joseph in the house of Potiphar and in prison, God was with Joseph now in the presence of Pharaoh. Joseph struggled and suffered for thirteen years. He endured arduous life reverses with a steady faithfulness to his God. Joseph did not allow his reverses to compromise his good character or his faith. Notice how Joseph conducted himself. He did not seek to, at this point, draw any attention to his plight or the injustices that have been perpetrated on him. Where, thinking logically, he would first of all plead his own case on his own behalf, he did not do that. Joseph said nothing about past injustice, he focused strictly on Pharaoh's issue, on Pharaoh's dreams.

Very quickly Joseph explained what Pharaoh has dreamed and he divulged the meaning of those two dreams. Quite simply Joseph shared with Pharaoh that there would be a seven year span of excellent bountiful crops. This seven year span of bounty would be followed by a seven year span of scarcity and famine. God graciously warned Pharaoh of these events. God showed mercy to this pagan King and his nation for the sake of Joseph and Joseph's family.

In addition, Joseph explained that the repetition of the dream signified that the matter is fixed and will happen quickly so the operative words here are action and haste. There is no time to lose. Preparation for the seven lean years must begin now during these seven good years. Now that the warning has been given to

Pharaoh Joseph approaches the issue practically under the wisdom and inspiration of God. Joseph encouraged Pharaoh to appoint a discerning and wise man over Egypt to administer their preparations for these events that God has warned Pharaoh of. It is not fair to suppose that Joseph was disingenuous here in devising Pharaoh that there needed to be a particular individual who is charged with this task of administration. There is none of the self-promotion he engaged in as a teenage boy. Joseph had been careful in his initial response to Pharaoh to give credit to God for any dream interpretation. By advising Pharaoh to select an individual to run this enterprise of collecting and storing excess crops, Joseph showed wisdom because this is going to be a full-time endeavor. Whoever has this position of authority will need to be able to focus their attention carefully on the task at hand.

The plan is to take twenty percent of the crop production for these seven years and set it aside. Please note this is not a tax per se or a biblical discussion on tax rates. There is a serious crisis at hand which requires careful planning if Egypt is to avoid mass starvation and social unrest. The fact that twenty percent is to be withheld, and not a greater percentage, is indicative of the size of the surplus that will be enjoyed in Egypt during this initial seven-year phase.

Intelligent frugality is just that: intelligent. As we have said before, God sees all of time in history and sees what is coming down the road. We of course, do not. Wisdom dictates that we reasonably and intelligently prepare for emergencies, for times of unexpected need. "Go to the ant, O sluggard; consider her ways, and be wise. Without having any chief, officer, or ruler she prepares her bread in summer and gathers her food in harvest." (Proverbs 6: 6-8 KJV). This is what my pastor as a youth used to call "sanctified common sense."

Our ultimate provider is the Lord; that goes without having to belabor the point too much. God doesn't promise to drop provision out of the sky if He has provided another avenue for us to meet our needs. God fed the Hebrews in the desert during the exodus because they had no way to provide food on a regular, on-going basis. Manna didn't fall from heaven in the Promised Land, however.

God would provide for Egypt but they still had a responsible role to play in that provision. Joseph is a part of that provision; the coming bumper-crops are part of that provision.

It is interesting to note that two dreams once almost led to Joseph's destruction, as we will see these two dreams lead to his exaltation.

CHAPTER TWENTY-THREE

ASCENSION

This proposal pleased Pharaoh and all his servants. And Pharaoh said to his servants, "Can we find a man like this, in whom is the Spirit of God?" Then Pharaoh said to Joseph, "Since God has shown you all this, there is none so discerning and wise as you are. You shall be over my house, and all my people shall order themselves as you command. Only as regards the throne will I be greater than you." And Pharaoh said to Joseph, "See, I have set you over all the land of Egypt." Then Pharaoh took his signet ring from his hand and put it on Joseph's hand, and clothed him in garments of fine linen and put a gold chain about his neck. And he made him ride in his second chariot. And they called out before him, "Bow the knee!" Thus he set him over all the land of Egypt. Moreover, Pharaoh said to Joseph, "I am Pharaoh, and without your consent no one shall lift up hand or foot in all the land of Egypt." And Pharaoh called Joseph's name Zaphenath-paneah. And he gave him in marriage Asenath, the daughter of Potiphera priest of On. So Joseph went out over the land of Egypt. Joseph was thirty years old when he entered the service of Pharaoh king of Egypt. And Joseph went out from the presence of Pharaoh and went through all the land of Egypt. During the seven plentiful years the earth produced abundantly, and he gathered up all the food of these seven years, which occurred in the land of Egypt, and put the food in the cities. He put in every city the food from the fields around it. And Joseph stored up grain in great abundance, like the sand of the sea, until he ceased to measure it, for it could not be measured. Before the year of famine came, two sons were born to Joseph. Asenath, the daughter of Potiphera priest of On, bore them to him. Joseph called the name of the first-born Manasseh. "For," he said, "God has made me forget all my hardship and all my father's house." The name of the second he called Ephraim, "For God has made me fruitful in the land of my affliction." The seven years of plenty that occurred in the land of Egypt came to an end, and the seven years of famine began to come, as Joseph had said. There was famine in all lands, but in all the land of Egypt there was bread. When all the land of Egypt was famished, the people cried to Pharaoh for bread. Pharaoh said to all the Egyptians, "Go to Joseph. What he says to you, do." So when the famine had spread over all the land, Joseph opened all the storehouses and sold to the Egyptians, for the famine was severe in the land of Egypt. Moreover, all the earth came to Egypt to Joseph to buy grain, because the famine was severe over all the earth. (Genesis 41: 37-57)

The LORD killeth, and maketh alive: he bringeth down to the grave, and bringeth up. The LORD maketh poor, and maketh rich: he bringeth low, and lifteth up. He raiseth up the poor out of the dust, and lifteth up the beggar from the dunghill, to set them among princes, and to make them inherit the throne of glory: for the pillars of the earth are the LORD's, and he hath set the world upon them. (1Samuel 2:6-8 KJV)

L ife can change with cataclysmic speed.

On April 12, 1945 Harry S Truman awoke as Vice President of the United States. It was, frankly a ceremonial position where his chief task was to preside over the Senate. Truman held no power and was woefully in the dark as to much of the deeper, more sensitive information and decisions of the war-time government. Previously a senator on a key committee to uncover fraud, waste and corruption in military contracts, Truman was bored. By eight o'clock on that evening of April 12, 1945, Truman would be President, after the death of Franklin Roosevelt. The next day President Truman told reporters he felt as if the sun, moon and stars had all fallen on him that day.[1]

The contrast for Joseph is far greater than that of Truman. It is astounding really to consider this day in Joseph's life. In the course of one day he went from a trustee in Pharaoh's jail to an interpreter of Pharaoh's dreams to Pharaoh's prime minister. Words fail to properly describe this shift in life.

It was time for Joseph to take up the task he had trained for these many years. Everywhere this excellent young man has been, he has responded to all situations, good and bad, with grace, ability, and wisdom. Now he will ascend to a position that makes Joseph the most powerful appointed official in the known world. He became the Vizier, the Grand Steward of Pharaoh's domain.

The position of Vizier was a known concept in Egypt, as ancient Egyptian text corroborate.[2] The Vizier's job was one of incredible authority and scope. So, on the one hand, it might be stunning to think that an individual outside of the then-current Egyptian government could be placed in such an exalted position. But this was not an isolated, one-time event.

---

1   David McCullough, *Truman* (New York: Simon & Schuster, 1992), 436.

2   See notation for verses 40, 41 in Genesis, chapter 41 in the ESV Study Bible: "A document in the tomb of Rekhmire in the late Bronze Age tells of the duties of Vizier in Egypt. He is the 'Grand Stewart of all Egypt' and all activities of state are under his control."

This was one particular occasion where it was good to be the messenger. Pharaoh was pleased, the text tells us, and he asked the court rhetorically if they can find another man like this filled with God's spirit. Pharaoh acknowledged that, in fact, God had revealed this explanation to Joseph. Still he deemed Joseph as discerning and wise, and then appointed Joseph as ruler over his house, second only to Pharaoh. The nation will be accountable to Joseph; his authority is immense and virtually total in scope.

Then Pharaoh placed on Joseph's finger his signet ring, his official ring with his seal. This seal functioned as a signature on official documents and carried the full weight of authority. The ring was power, plain and simple.

Joseph was clothed in fine clothing with jewelry as fitting for his station, a further mark of his authority. Earlier in his life, fine clothing was a token of a family position he could not legitimately hold (through no fault of his own). The clothing had been yanked off his body. Then, he had lost clothing fitting for his station as manager of Potiphar's house to avoid adultery. Now he is clothed in fine clothing once more, but this is now his, properly, and legitimately. Joseph is provided his own chariot and Egypt moves at his command.

It is perfectly reasonable to wonder what the household of Potiphar thought of Joseph's ascension. It would be no stretch of credulity to think that Potiphar's wife was nervous. The way of this world is to utilize power to settle old scores but, as we will see, that is not Joseph's way.

Joseph received a new, Egyptian name: Zaphenath-peneah; he is given a woman, Asenath who is the daughter of a priest as his wife. This integrated Joseph fully into Pharaoh's court, giving him important family connections and helping to legitimize his position.

We are told that Joseph is now thirty years of age. He is no longer a boy but fully a man. Once a slave and then a prisoner, he can now roam all over Egypt as he pleases. Quickly he set about the task of gathering grain and storing it in cities during the seven abundant years. The crops are exceptional so Joseph stored them carefully. In this good time Asenath gives him two sons as well.

The seven years pass and now the famine arrived as foretold. Joseph sold grain to the Egyptians as the famine worsens and people from other nations travel to Egypt because the famine is widespread. The famine reaches into Canaan as well.

CHAPTER TWENTY-FOUR

UNEXPECTED CUSTOMERS

When Jacob learned that there was grain for sale in Egypt, he said to his sons, "Why do you look at one another?" And he said, "Behold, I have heard that there is grain for sale in Egypt. Go down and buy grain for us there, that we may live and not die." So ten of Joseph's brothers went down to buy grain in Egypt. But Jacob did not send Benjamin, Joseph's brother, with his brothers, for he feared that harm might happen to him. Thus the sons of Israel came to buy among the others who came, for the famine was in the land of Canaan. Now Joseph was governor over the land. He was the one who sold to all the people of the land. And Joseph's brothers came and bowed themselves before him with their faces to the ground. Joseph saw his brothers and recognized them, but he treated them like strangers and spoke roughly to them. "Where do you come from?" he said. They said, "From the land of Canaan, to buy food." And Joseph recognized his brothers, but they did not recognize him. (Genesis 42: 1-8)

The famine that has struck the known world becomes increasingly severe. Now our story shifts back once again to the household of Jacob and his eleven sons. The famine obviously had now hit Canaan and the situation was getting dire. Jacob, an intelligent man and administrator, always had his ear to the ground to learn what was going on in the world around him. Word came to Jacob that grain was being sold in Egypt. His words to the sons were somewhat comical, "Why are you guys all standing around looking at each other? Do something! Go to Egypt and buy grain," is the gist of his words. It is almost as if Jacob was chiding them for lack of initiative and inactivity. His words made it clear that they must act or face starvation. Starvation, the threat of it at least, is an enormous motivator. Perhaps a point we can take away from this is that faith in God stifles neither initiative nor wise self-responsibility. God provides for us yet his provision most frequently is an opportunity. God's provision for Jacob's clan is the grain that is in Egypt but God is not going to transport the grain from Egypt to Canaan for them. They must go purchase it; they must act.

Jacob sent ten of his sons down to Egypt but not Benjamin. The text makes it clear that Jacob feared for his youngest child's safety. We certainly do wonder with reason if Jacob had nagging doubts and suspicions that he could not dismiss about Joseph's fate. As we can tell, Benjamin has, somewhat, taken the place of Joseph, as the favored child. Jacob did not want to repeat the utter agony of soul that he endured in the loss of Joseph.

For those who have suffered the loss of a loved one, it produces a wound to the soul. That wound may scab over, and for most of us who have losses, mercifully it does. Yet the reminder that is emotional scar tissue does not go away after a loss. Faith can make severe loss bearable but faith does not negate suffering. Jacob's heart was scarred. Mark Twain recounted in his autobiography how, when he learned of the death of his daughter Jean, he said, "Now I know how a soldier feels when a bullet pierces his heart."[1] Jacob's heart had been pierced.

The sons of Jacob came down to meet with the governor of Egypt to buy grain. The governor, or the Vizier, was the one who sold the grain. Of course, as we are reminded, Joseph was the governor. Joseph met with those who came down to purchase the grain. On this particular day he was conducting his business when Joseph received a shock. There standing before Joseph were the ten brothers who betrayed him and sold him into slavery twenty-two years prior.

These same men, who had so cruelly treated him and with total and callous disregard now came before him, and bowed down with their faces to the ground. We can scarcely begin to imagine the emotions that rushed through Joseph's heart as they lay before him in an act of total submission. "[He] saw his brothers and recognized them..." (Verse 7).

Joseph pretended not to know them and he spoke roughly to them, querying them as to where they were from. Of course he wanted to make sure that he has identified them correctly. He knows in his heart, yet he wants to make sure and they tell him that they are from the land of Canaan and that they have come to buy food. Their identity was now a certainty.

What we now read in verse eight of our text was a reiteration of Joseph's recognition of them but an important detail is added that is critical to our story: the ten brothers did not recognize Joseph. There is no reason to doubt the biblical narrative here. When Judah hatched his nefarious plan to sell Joseph, he and his nine other brothers were all adult men. They were bearded and had a certain manner of dress and speech. Twenty years pass, they still are bearded and look essentially the same, just older, grayer but with still the same manner of dress and speaking their particular language.

Contrast this to Joseph now. Twenty years have passed but

---

1   Samuel Clemons, ed. Charles Neider, *The Autobiography of Mark Twain* (New York: Harper and Row, 1959), 582.

when they last saw him, he was essentially a boy. Now he is a mature man close to forty years of age. He was clean-shaven, as was the Egyptian custom, dressed as an Egyptian and speaking to them (as we will see) in the Egyptian language through an interpreter. So stealth was on the side of Joseph and he had them at a disadvantage.

In the Peter Jackson film, *The Hobbit: An Unexpected Journey*, there is the scene where Biblo Baggins is escaping from Gollum after finding the ring. As it happens, Gollum is standing between Bilbo and the mouth of the cave. To escape, Bilbo must get by Gollum. Bilbo is wearing the ring and he is invisible. The hobbit could easily stab and kill the pitiful Gollum but he instead leaps over Gollum and escapes. It is as Gandalf would later say that "… pity stayed [Bilbo's] hand." This encapsulates our scenario here between Joseph and these cruel brothers; they had no idea who they were dealing with; all they saw is an Egyptian official, not a brother thought dead. Joseph could have had them executed on the spot, but undeserved mercy stayed his hand.

CHAPTER TWENTY-FIVE

A DISTANT DREAM

And Joseph remembered the dreams that he had dreamed of them. And he said to them, "You are spies; you have come to see the nakedness of the land." They said to him, "No, my lord, your servants have come to buy food. We are all sons of one man. We are honest men. Your servants have never been spies." He said to them, "No, it is the nakedness of the land that you have come to see." And they said, "We, your servants, are twelve brothers, the sons of one man in the land of Canaan, and behold, the youngest is this day with our father, and one is no more." But Joseph said to them, "It is as I said to you. You are spies. By this you shall be tested: by the life of Pharaoh, you shall not go from this place unless your youngest brother comes here. Send one of you, and let him bring your brother, while you remain confined, that your words may be tested, whether there is truth in you. Or else, by the life of Pharaoh, surely you are spies." And he put them all together in custody for three days. (Genesis 42: 9-17)

The memory of his dreams all those years prior must have struck Joseph forcibly as he beheld his brothers on the ground in obeisance toward him. As we have said Joseph, could have had them slain on the spot and who would have called his actions in the question? His power and authority was that great. A true test of character for all of us is how we treat those whom we are in a position of authority and control over. In Ephesians chapter 6, Paul makes very clear to the people of his day who were masters or owners of slaves that they had a responsibility in how they treated those under them. Paul reminded the owners of slaves, of those in authority over others that they themselves have one who is in authority over them, one whom they also will give an account to and must submit to. To be sure, if there was ever anyone who had a score to settle with others, it was Joseph with his ten brothers. But as we will see later, Joseph knew that his brothers ultimately were not accountable to him, but to God Almighty.

Joseph's immediate response toward his brothers was, on the face of it, harsh and accusatory. He deemed them as foreign spies come to scout the land for possible invasion. Obviously this is a serious charge and a potentially deadly accusation as spies, tend to be executed. So the brothers knew immediately that their lives were in great danger. This was not going as they had supposed. They most likely imagined they would come in, conduct their business, and leave but now they are receiving most unwelcome attention from the Vizier of Egypt, a man who literally holds their lives in his hands. Their integrity, their trustworthiness, was being called into question by a man, insofar as they know, they have never met. But we know that he, in fact, knew them all too well. He had suffered greatly at their hands and the simple fact is he did not trust them. Indeed for Joseph to trust them at this point would have been extremely foolish.

Perhaps some of Joseph harshness toward his brothers was to mask what had to be a maelstrom of emotions surging within him. He will react strongly and emotionally to some statements that they make, as the text show us. As frightened as these ten sons of Jacob must have been, Joseph was dealing with strong emotions as well. There's no way around the fact that the arrival of these men must have stirred up many difficult and painful memories. Doubtless, Joseph was trying very hard to keep it all together emotionally and maintain his composure.

So the ten brothers defended themselves. They told Joseph that they were members of the household of twelve sons of their father. They further elaborated that they were from Canaan and that two brothers are not with them. They advised Joseph that one of their brothers was with their father and that another brother was dead, of course having no idea that they are addressing the brother whom they thought lay as cold bones in some unmarked slave-pit.

To Joseph the words were telling, insofar as he was able to determine his brother Benjamin and his father were still alive. We cannot help but wonder if Joseph had not feared for the life of his brother Benjamin, as Benjamin too was a favorite of his father's. Now he heard that Benjamin is alive.

Once again Joseph accused them of being spies and he told them that they will all be imprisoned, save one, and that that individual will go back and retrieve Benjamin to return to Egypt. He informed them that this will prove that they were telling the truth if Benjamin is returned. Joseph had them all put in jail for three days. Literally and figuratively Joseph, sweated his brothers.

CHAPTER TWENTY-SIX

A GUILTY ADMISSION

On the third day Joseph said to them, "Do this and you will live, for I fear God: if you are honest men, let one of your brothers remain confined where you are in custody, and let the rest go and carry grain for the famine of your households, and bring your youngest brother to me. So your words will be verified, and you shall not die." And they did so. Then they said to one another, "In truth we are guilty concerning our brother, in that we saw the distress of his soul, when he begged us and we did not listen. That is why this distress has come upon us." And Reuben answered them, "Did I not tell you not to sin against the boy? But you did not listen. So now there comes a reckoning for his blood." They did not know that Joseph understood them, for there was an interpreter between them. Then he turned away from them and wept. And he returned to them and spoke to them. And he took Simeon from them and bound him before their eyes. (Genesis 42:18-24)

After three days Joseph had his brothers released from prison and brought before him. He told them that he too feared

God and that he has had a change in mind as to how he will address their situation. Now all but one will return to Canaan and one will stay as his prisoner until the return of the nine brothers, with Benjamin. It does not seem that this was a change of mind for Joseph but rather a plan that he had decided to carefully execute. Joseph wanted to see what the current and true nature of his brothers was. He wanted to see if they are still the same men that sold him as a slave twenty-two years prior. He wanted to know if there has been a change of heart; if they are trustworthy. He wanted to know if they have come to regret their actions. It seems probable as well that Joseph knew that his father would not allow all of his sons to remain in custody in Egypt and then send Benjamin, his last remaining child, down to where his other sons were being held. It would seem logical that Joseph's actual plan all along was to detain one and send the other's home with the instruction that when they return, Benjamin must accompany them.

Joseph wanted to see his little brother but he also wanted to determine that the brothers were telling the truth that Benjamin was alive and well. Also he probably wanted to see how his brothers were treating Benjamin without them knowing who Joseph was. Joseph knew that much would be explained in the treatment of Benjamin by these brothers.

It is here that the narrative takes an interesting turn. We would think that the brothers would be greatly relieved that they had been released and will be allowed to return home as quickly and quietly as possible. In fact, the ten brothers began to accuse each other, that their troubles were a result of their earlier mistreatment of Joseph. They said this to each other that all of this came through their own fault. They deserved these troubles because they ignored the cries and the pleas for mercy from their brother Joseph.

What a startling admission that they made in front of the presence of the court. To be sure they were speaking Hebrew and thought that their conversation was largely unheeded, never thinking that the Egyptian would understand their words. These men were plagued with guilt; they now felt the full weight of the responsibility of their actions towards Joseph and they regretted their actions deeply. As we have said previously these men were not sociopaths. These brothers all had a conscience and their consciences accused them day and night for years of the terrible, terrible thing that they had done. Their very real guilt was eating them alive. The ten brothers felt now that justice was being served upon them. Reuben spoke up and he blamed them specifically for not listening to him and sparing the boy.

On the morning of April 15, 1912 reports began to circulate across the world that the Ocean liner Titanic, a marvel of engineering and opulence had struck an iceberg and sank. The ship was deemed, with hubris, as 'unsinkable' but it was not and it floundered on its maiden voyage. The loss of life was immense. The worst, most far reaching design flaw was that the lifeboats could only hold half of the compliment of the ship. Far less than half were saved.[1]

What enraged the public was that although the practice essentially followed due to social dictum on a sinking vessel was 'women and children first' into the lifeboats it was determined that the owner of the cruise line, J Bruce Ismay, had saved himself taking a space in one of the lifeboats. To many his actions were craven and unmanly and he lived out his life in disgrace. He was adjudged guilty as a coward. Ismay professed no guilt for either his actions in saving himself or the lack of lifeboats on the doomed ocean liner. The public did not agree and condemned Ismay's actions.

The events of November 22, 1963 traumatized our country as no other event, save perhaps September 11, 2001. We were a different people then, in some ways more unscarred, more innocent. The loss of President Kennedy to an assassin's bullet was the

---

1   Walter Lord, *A Night to Remember* (New York: Henry Holt and Company, 1955), 109, 172. Also see F. Wilson, "J Bruce Ismay: doomed the moment he jumped ship," *The Telegraph*, online ed. 8/3/2011.

start, seemingly, of the slide into the dark turbulent decade of the 60's. Our country would never be the same.

There was not only a collective sense of grief there was some collective feelings of guilt, that there was a previously undiagnosed pathology in the psyche of our country that gave rise to a Lee Harvey Oswald. For some, close to the events of that day, the sense of guilt was pervasive and very real.

When the shots rang out in Dealey plaza one Secret Service agent responded to the gunfire and moved to reach the presidential limousine and hopefully shield the president with his own body. That agent who reacted was Clint Hill, actually assigned to protect Jackie Kennedy. Agent Hill was scant seconds too late, the fatal shot already found its mark. Hill did manage to get on the car and push Mrs. Kennedy back into her seat and rode atop the limousine to Parkland Hospital, shielding the First Lady and the President from view.

Clint Hill initially felt he could have done more and blamed himself for not acting quickly enough. He had acted bravely but the distance too great and the assassin had the advantage. He was judged a hero in everyone's mind but his own. He felt a terrible sense of guilt.[2]

Guilt and true culpability do not always go hand in hand but Joseph's brothers were culpable and they did feel guilty.

Joseph, of course, heard and understood all that was said. Joseph spoke to his brothers through an interpreter to disguise himself. Consequently, they logically assumed that he did not understand their language so they felt free to discuss these matters in front of him. But Joseph understood exactly what was said and he could not easily contain or control his emotions. Joseph left them and wept. It may be that Joseph wept once again for the betrayal, the rejection and the suffering at the hands of his brothers. It may also be that Joseph wept tears of sorrow inter-

---

2   Gerald Blaine & Lisa McCubbin, *The President's Detail: JFK's Secret Service Agents Break Their Silence* (New York: Gallery Books, 2010). Kindle ed. chapters 12, 18, 24.

mingled with tears of joy because he learned now that these men felt a great sense of responsibility and guilt over their actions so many years ago. Joseph still has to learn more completely about their character and where they are functioning as men, but he now knew that there is some possibility that he can restore a relationship with them. But the time was not yet right for that relationship; their character required testing. Joseph must see that these are truly changed, contrite men. So he had Simeon bound before them as a hostage. Nine brothers started out on a journey to return home to their land and to their father.

CHAPTER TWENTY-SEVEN

"ALL THIS HAS COME AGAINST ME."

And Joseph gave orders to fill their bags with grain, and to replace every man's money in his sack, and to give them provisions for the journey. This was done for them. Then they loaded their donkeys with their grain and departed. And as one of them opened his sack to give his donkey fodder at the lodging place, he saw his money in the mouth of his sack. He said to his brothers, "My money has been put back; here it is in the mouth of my sack!" At this their hearts failed them, and they turned trembling to one another, saying, "What is this that God has done to us?" When they came to Jacob their father in the land of Canaan, they told him all that had happened to them, saying, "The man, the lord of the land, spoke roughly to us and took us to be spies of the land. But we said to him, 'We are honest men; we have never been spies. We are twelve brothers, sons of our father. One is no more, and the youngest is this day with our father in the land of Canaan.' Then the man, the lord of the land, said to us, 'By this I shall know that you are honest men: leave one of your brothers with me, and take grain for the famine of your households, and go your way.

Bring your youngest brother to me. Then I shall know that you are not spies but honest men, and I will deliver your brother to you, and you shall trade in the land." As they emptied their sacks, behold, every man's bundle of money was in his sack. And when they and their father saw their bundles of money, they were afraid. And Jacob their father said to them, "You have bereaved me of my children: Joseph is no more, and Simeon is no more, and now you would take Benjamin. All this has come against me." Then Reuben said to his father, "Kill my two sons if I do not bring him back to you. Put him in my hands, and I will bring him back to you." But he said, "My son shall not go down with you, for his brother is dead, and he is the only one left. If harm should happen to him on the journey that you are to make, you would bring down my gray hairs with sorrow to Sheol." (Genesis 42: 25-38)

Although Joseph spoke roughly to these men and although he imprisoned one of their own, the tone of speech and treatment of Joseph did not show his true intentions. Joseph was testing them carefully. Although he has heard them admit among themselves that their treatment of him was terrible Joseph was perceptive enough to see that an admission of guilt did not necessarily equate to a change in behavior. Joseph's intentions were to test his brothers with thorough planning and patience.

Joseph was not dealing with forgiveness here per se. Rather he was seeking to determine if there was any basis on which he could rebuild a relationship with them.

Forgive and forget is not always the wisest and best policy in human relationships. Oh we should always forgive; we have seen forgiveness is commanded, it is a requirement of our faith walk, not an option. Forgive, yes, but it is not necessarily wise to forget. Healthy relationships require an open trust and a level of vulnerability to another person or persons. It is that vulnerability that can become problematic if we open ourselves to someone who is physically and emotionally destructive. The apostle Paul gave us wise words, "If possible, so far as it depends on you, live peaceably with all." (Romans 12:18). There are some people that we cannot live peaceably with.

If a person has broken faith with us, if they have broken the peace and have done us wrong wisdom may well dictate that we test them carefully to see whether there is true repentance and true change or not. Testing an individual carefully is important in determining if proper boundaries will, in fact, be respected.

Joseph has and will be taking steps to determine the genuineness of repentance in the lives of his brothers. It would seem that his concern was not physical. After all he is the second most important individual in Egypt and there would be nothing to be gained by them on any act of violence. Doubtless too, he had bodyguards. The issue is violence to his heart and soul by further betrayal and unrepentant actions of these ten men.

Even as he went about testing his brothers he still showed them grace. The money that they brought to pay for grain he returned to them and there is no reason to think that this was anything other than an act of kindness on Joseph's part. Joseph's act of kindness had unintended consequences with his brothers who were traveling home. When one of the ten brothers finds his payment in his sack of grain, returned to him the response of the men is one of fear. Their guilty consciences were speaking against them and accusing them. They fear that it is a judgment from God. Certainly they knew they deserved punishment from God and perhaps they felt that the chickens, at last, had come home to roost. They also feared that this was a deliberate act, to use as a pretext for some plot against them.

So the weary travelers arrived at home and they shared with their father Jacob all that had transpired. They explained how the Governor of Egypt had been harsh and accusatory. They recounted how they had, in their defense, told the Egyptian ruler that they were honest men originally of a family of twelve sons. One was dead and another, the youngest, with their father. They told Jacob how this man in Egypt had demanded that they bring Benjamin down to Egypt to prove their innocence, to prove their word that they were not spies.

Then the brothers all opened up their sacks and found each of them their money returned. It frightened Jacob and his clan because the money gave the appearance that the grain was not paid for as agreed--that it is even stolen. Jacob then enumerated to his remaining sons that Simeon is in prison Joseph is dead and that Benjamin must be sent down with them to buy more grain, "All this has come against me." Jacob chose to interpret the events in front of them in the worst of all possible ways. Jacob drew a conclusion without having all the facts at his disposal.

Jacob's misinterpretation of the events is instructive for us. Now, on one level, his apprehension is understandable. For all intents and purposes he has lost one son that he knows of and potentially another. Now he faces the possible loss of his youngest child who is a favorite. Of course we have Scripture that declares God's intentions toward us, scripture that Jacob did not have. That being said, Jacob was still not accurately considering his own personal past and his relationship with God. Jacob knew that God had blessed his life and touched it in an amazing way and that God had made promises to him about his future and the future of his children. But, as we all are, Jacob was dust with all of the frailties inherent therein. At this point Jacob did not consider God's promises for the future; he focused on losses both real and imagined. At this time Jacob did not have eyes to see the work of God in these distressing events in his life.

We're so blessed; we have all of Scripture to encourage us. Each time in his life that Joseph faced a major life reversal or setback we read the testimony of Scripture that "... the Lord was with Joseph." Although circumstances were dire God did not abandon Joseph when he went to the house of Potiphar and God did not abandon Joseph when he was placed in prison. It all seems contradictory when you consider it: Joseph suffers yet God is with him.

What we take away from this is that God was with Joseph in the suffering and we can take away for ourselves the same lesson. Circumstances are usually momentary and temporal. Circumstances change but God's love for us and His good intentions toward us are never negated by circumstances. Indeed current circumstances do not necessarily convey God's intentions toward us long term.

But Jacob cannot see the hand of God in his present circumstances. He is not at a point where he will willingly send Benjamin down with the brothers so that they can buy more grain. Jacob has not resolved his character flaw; he is still playing favorites. He will not risk losing Benjamin.

The words of Matthew Henry are wise:

> ...we often perplex ourselves with our own mistakes, even in matters of fact. True griefs may arise from false intelligence and suppositions. Jacob gives up Joseph for gone, and Simeon and Benjamin as being in danger; and he concludes, All these things are against me. It proved otherwise, that all these were for him, were working together for his good and the good of his family: yet here he thinks them all against him. Note, Through our ignorance and mistake, and the weakness of our faith, we often apprehend that to be against us which is really for us. We are afflicted in body, estate, name, and relations; and we think all these things are against us, whereas these are really working for us the weight of glory.[1]

---

1   Matthew Henry, 84.

Chapter Twenty-eight

A Second Journey to Egypt

Now the famine was severe in the land. And when they had eaten the grain that they had brought from Egypt, their father said to them, "Go again, buy us a little food." But Judah said to him, "The man solemnly warned us, saying, 'You shall not see my face unless your brother is with you.' If you will send our brother with us, we will go down and buy you food. But if you will not send him, we will not go down, for the man said to us, 'You shall not see my face, unless your brother is with you.'" Israel said, "Why did you treat me so badly as to tell the man that you had another brother?" They replied, "The man questioned us carefully about ourselves and our kindred, saying, 'Is your father still alive? Do you have another brother?' What we told him was in answer to these questions. Could we in any way know that he would say, 'Bring your brother down'?" And Judah said to Israel his father, "Send the boy with me, and we will arise and go, that we may live and not die, both we and you and also our little ones. I will be a pledge of his safety. From my hand you shall require him. If I do not bring him back to you and set him before you, then let me

bear the blame forever. If we had not delayed, we would
now have returned twice." Then their father Israel said to
them, "If it must be so, then do this: take some of the choice
fruits of the land in your bags, and carry a present down
to the man, a little balm and a little honey, gum, myrrh,
pistachio nuts, and almonds. Take double the money with
you. Carry back with you the money that was returned in
the mouth of your sacks. Perhaps it was an oversight. Take
also your brother, and arise, go again to the man. May
God Almighty grant you mercy before the man, and may
he send back your other brother and Benjamin. And as for
me, if I am bereaved of my children, I am bereaved." So
the men took this present, and they took double the money
with them, and Benjamin. They arose and went down to
Egypt and stood before Joseph. (Genesis 43:1-15)

Over an indeterminate period of time the family of Jacob
ate the food brought back from Egypt and once again they
found themselves in dire straits. The famine continued so there
is no other choice than for the sons of Jacob to travel to Egypt
once again and purchase grain. So Jacob instructed the sons to
return, to journey back to Egypt. At this point Judah reminded his father that unless they bring Benjamin with them, they
will not see the governor to purchase grain. Benjamin's presence
with them is a non-negotiable item. It had been made clear to
them, that what was considered proof that they were not spies
would be that Benjamin traveled with them, and was presented
to this ruler. To the tribe of Jacob, on the face of it, this probably
made no sense that Benjamin had to come along. Of course they
did not have all the facts of their disposal: the knowledge of who
the governor was, that he was Joseph thought long-lost.

There were reasons for Joseph wanting to see Benjamin some
obvious and some probably a supposition. Certainly he wanted
to see his younger brother, which is the most obvious reason.
But perhaps he wanted to make sure that Benjamin was well and

that the brothers did not have designs on Benjamin's life. Perhaps it is well he wanted to make sure that the brothers were not lying about whether Benjamin was alive or not. Joseph certainly had reason to wonder as to how they might have treated Benjamin in the intervening years. If the nine brothers return to Egypt with no Benjamin and tried to explain away his absence by an early death or some mischief then Joseph would have learned everything he needed to know about his brothers. He needed verifiable evidence, as much as he could get it, that they were truthful and were telling the truth.

When Jacob is reminded that Benjamin must travel also he got upset, complaining that the brothers made matters worse by mentioning the existence of Benjamin. Of course the brothers had no earthly idea why they were so closely queried about their father and about any other brothers; they had answered the questions truthfully enough not suspecting that the existence of Benjamin would become a real issue. They saw no apparent reason to be evasive, never guessing that Joseph would require Benjamin to accompany them back to Egypt.

The brothers explained to their father that this unexpected line of questioning and the results caught them off guard but now they have no choice. Judah's response was most telling. Judah made a pledge for the safe return of Benjamin and accepted full responsibility for Benjamin. That Judah is willing to guarantee Benjamin safety is a major point in our story. Remember Judah was the one who came up with the idea to sell Joseph into slavery but as we will see this is no longer that same Judah. At this Jacob relented. Jacob sent with his sons gifts for the governor. He also sent the original purchase price in money for the first shipment plus money to cover this one. Jacob's plan was to smooth over any misunderstanding or possible ill feelings that there might be between the family of Jacob and this harsh Egyptian governor. Jacob asked for the mercy of Almighty God, of the El' Shaddai, and resigned himself to what ever will transpire when Benjamin gets to Egypt.

CHAPTER TWENTY-NINE

BENJAMIN

When Joseph saw Benjamin with them, he said to the steward of his house, "Bring the men into the house, and slaughter an animal and make ready, for the men are to dine with me at noon." The man did as Joseph told him and brought the men to Joseph's house. And the men were afraid because they were brought to Joseph's house, and they said, "It is because of the money, which was replaced in our sacks the first time, that we are brought in, so that he may assault us and fall upon us to make us servants and seize our donkeys." So they went up to the steward of Joseph's house and spoke with him at the door of the house, and said, "Oh, my lord, we came down the first time to buy food. And when we came to the lodging place we opened our sacks, and there was each man's money in the mouth of his sack, our money in full weight. So we have brought it again with us, and we have brought other money down with us to buy food. We do not know who put our money in our sacks." He replied, "Peace to you, do not be afraid. Your God and the God of your father has put treasure in your sacks for you. I received your money." Then he brought

Simeon out to them. And when the man had brought the
men into Joseph's house and given them water, and they
had washed their feet, and when he had given their don-
keys fodder, they prepared the present for Joseph's coming
at noon, for they heard that they should eat bread there.
When Joseph came home, they brought into the house to
him the present that they had with them and bowed down
to him to the ground. And he inquired about their welfare
and said, "Is your father well, the old man of whom you
spoke? Is he still alive?" They said, "Your servant our father
is well; he is still alive." And they bowed their heads and
prostrated themselves. And he lifted up his eyes and saw
his brother Benjamin, his mother's son, and said, "Is this
your youngest brother, of whom you spoke to me? God be
gracious to you, my son!" Then Joseph hurried out, for his
compassion grew warm for his brother, and he sought a
place to weep. And he entered his chamber and wept there.
Then he washed his face and came out. And controlling
himself he said, "Serve the food." They served him by him-
self, and them by themselves, and the Egyptians who ate
with him by themselves, because the Egyptians could not
eat with the Hebrews, for that is an abomination to the
Egyptians. And they sat before him, the firstborn according
to his birthright and the youngest according to his youth.
And the men looked at one another in amazement. Por-
tions were taken to them from Joseph's table, but Benja-
min's portion was five times as much as any of theirs. And
they drank and were merry with him. (Genesis 43:16-34)

As we read through the narrative here and following into
chapter 44 of Genesis it is difficult to come to any other
conclusion than that Joseph had planned out very carefully what
he would do when the brothers returned for more grain. These
events show the mark of a careful planner and administrator. We
may wonder what Joseph thought as he waited for his brothers to

return. And would they return? Or would they consider Simeon collateral damage.

We are told that when Joseph saw Benjamin he arranged a luncheon for his brothers to be held that very day. Doubtless this was a planned move and it is not unreasonable to conjecture that if in fact Benjamin had not been with them that Joseph would have broken off contact and ended the matter there. Unknown to Benjamin he was the linchpin in this whole matter. Joseph will surmise much of current attitudes and intentions of his brother based on Benjamin.

So these ten sons of Jacob are escorted to the house of Joseph. Far from setting their mind at ease, the invitation filled them with dread and fear. Well they remembered their first visit and it was most definitely not a pleasant affair. They had been accused of being spies; one of their own had been taken from them, bound and placed in prison. Further demands were made on them as conditions for further trade which was bringing their youngest brother with them. Doubtless it was all perplexing and disturbing to the brothers and we cannot blame them for feeling this way. So here they go to Joseph's house and they are afraid, frankly, that it is a ruse, a trap. The sons of Jacob believed that all of this related back to their first trip when they all ended up going home with the money brought to pay for the grain. They had been accused of being spies. Now, doubtless, they were afraid they will be deemed thieves. The brothers were afraid that they were going to be attacked, seized, forcibly made slaves and their animals confiscated. They were as about as anxious as anyone can be.

All of that being said, the brothers did act wisely now. They went to the steward of Joseph's house and they explained to him what had happened previously with the money they had brought for payment. The brothers wanted to smooth this issue over and clear up any misunderstandings that may have resulted from these events. The response of the steward was most gracious. "Peace to you, do not be afraid. Your God and the God of your father has put treasure in your sacks for you. I received your money." (Genesis 43:23)

"Your God and the God of your father...." What a powerful statement the steward makes here, for he alluded not to the gods of Egypt and to their pantheon but to the brothers' God and the God of their father. This can be no other God than Yahweh-God. These sons probably wandered how this Egyptian knew about their God? Well, the most logical explanation would be from our vantage point that Joseph had shared with his household about the God whom he served. It would be puzzling to the sons of Jacob, because as far as they knew they were dealing with a native Egyptian who did not worship Yahweh-God.

But here they are in a foreign land, in a heathen nation and their God is being honored and praised as the one whom has done good to them, as the one who has blessed them. Remember when we spoke of Jacob in the previous chapter, how he interpreted the events surrounding the detaining of Simeon, the accusation of being spies and the demand for Benjamin as proof that God was against him. But God was for him; God was for these brothers just as he was for Joseph. We have a lesson encapsulated in the words of the hymn from William Cowper: "Judge not the Lord by feeble sense, but trust Him for His grace; behind a frowning providence He hides a smiling face."[1]

For Jacob and his sons, the Providence of God does seem to be frowning; His Providence does seem to be dark. But there is a smiling face behind those dark clouds. There is mercy, kindness, grace and provision in these events. These men felt guilty for what they did to Joseph, all those years ago. Their guilt ate at them. They looked at these events which they did not understand and they feared they were in judgment because, deep down, they knew that they deserved judgment and punishment. Joseph was in a position to judge them and make them pay for

---

1   William Cowper, "God Moves in a Mysterious Way," a hymn, (public domain, 1774).

their crimes and who would stay his hand? Pharaoh? Doubtless, if Joseph had explained to Pharaoh his history with these brothers, there would have been no interference whatsoever. Joseph, as we will see, will show mercy.

When Joseph came home his brothers once again bowed down to him as a sign of their respect. When he was a youth, Joseph dreamed twice that his brothers would bow to him and now that had transpired; his dreams had been fulfilled. Joseph carefully inquired of his father and his father's health. Doubtless, he is filled with joy to know that his father was still alive. Then he sees his brother Benjamin for the first time in 22 years. Benjamin was not a child anymore but was a man. He was Joseph's full-blood relative and Joseph's heart was moved toward him. The Scripture tells us that his compassion grew warm toward his brother that his emotions were heightened and he left them because he could not maintain his composure in front of them. Without this interlude he could not maintain the charade that he had so carefully constructed up to this point. Joseph went where he could weep. Under the gruff exterior that Joseph has shown to his brothers there was an abiding sense of tenderness and kindness. That Joseph went to weep gives us further clues, even at this point, as to his intentions toward his brothers. Although previously he had been angry and accusatory his true demeanor toward his brothers was one of grace and kindness; he was not looking for vengeance. He was not looking to settle a score with these brothers. He did not rage at them no, his emotional response was weeping.

After a period of great emotion in private, Joseph washed his face to erase as best he could the evidence of his tears and lunch was served. As was the Egyptian custom Joseph did not eat at the table with his brothers, it would have been scandalous behavior for him to do so. Joseph still maintained something of a charade that he might fully test his brothers so he wanted them to consider him Egyptian. What Joseph did astonished his eleven brothers. He set their seating based on birth-order. How could he have known this? Benjamin, shown favor, was given far more food than the other brothers in his portions.

What was Joseph doing here? Certainly this table arrangement rocked them all back on their heels and doubtless conveyed the idea that Joseph was remarkably prescient. It implied more than ordinary power and made Joseph all the more intimidating. Regardless, Joseph was a good host and they had a good meal and a good time at his table. Doubtless, the brothers believed they had turned a corner in their relationship with this seemingly prickly Egyptian.

CHAPTER THIRTY

THE SILVER CUP

Then he commanded the steward of his house, "Fill the men's sacks with food, as much as they can carry, and put each man's money in the mouth of his sack, and put my cup, the silver cup, in the mouth of the sack of the youngest, with his money for the grain." And he did as Joseph told him. As soon as the morning was light, the men were sent away with their donkeys. They had gone only a short distance from the city. Now Joseph said to his steward, "Up, follow after the men, and when you overtake them, say to them, 'Why have you repaid evil for good? Is it not from this that my lord drinks, and by this that he practices divination? You have done evil in doing this.'" When he overtook them, he spoke to them these words. They said to him, "Why does my lord speak such words as these? Far be it from your servants to do such a thing! Behold, the money that we found in the mouths of our sacks we brought back to you from the land of Canaan. How then could we steal silver or gold from your lord's house? Whichever of your servants is found with it shall die, and we also will be my lord's servants." He said, "Let it be as you say: he

who is found with it shall be my servant, and the rest of
you shall be innocent." Then each man quickly lowered his
sack to the ground, and each man opened his sack. And
he searched, beginning with the eldest and ending with the
youngest. And the cup was found in Benjamin's sack. Then
they tore their clothes, and every man loaded his donkey,
and they returned to the city. (Genesis 44:1-13)

Now Joseph acted to test his brothers in a very difficult and severe situation. Joseph instructed the steward to replace his brother's money in the mouth of the sacks of grain that they're going to take back to Canaan. It is a repeat of the kindness he showed them previously when they came to get grain the first time. However Joseph provided additional instructions. The Stewart was told to take Joseph's silver cup and to place it in the mouth of the sack of the youngest brother, who of course, is Benjamin.

At first light, the eleven sons of Jacob start their journey home. They had only gone a short distance when Joseph pulled aside the Stewart and told him to pursue his brothers and when he overtook them to accuse them of stealing his silver cup, the cup supposedly that he used for divination. Saying that the silver cup was used for an occult practice was a part of the ruse, part of the drama that Joseph deliberately created here.

The steward did as instructed by Joseph and when accused, the brothers were indignant. They have not only been accused of theft, they have also been accused of tremendous ingratitude, taking advantage of a host and his good nature. Essentially they were accused of spitting in the hand extended in friendship. Now these brothers knew that they are innocent of such a charge and so they protested their innocence. They reminded the steward about the money they had found previously squirreled away in their sacks, from the first trip, they had returned along with more money and gifts to show their good intent. And so the brothers, declaring their innocence, say that whoever is found guilty of such a crime should be put to death and they, the other brothers, become slaves to Joseph. They were so confident of their own innocence that they create a potentially terrible scenario of punishment, but they are innocent men of this crime. It is interesting to note that although the brothers offered up the life of the guilty party as payment for the crime the steward declared a lesser punishment for the offender. The thief will become a slave to Joseph and the others will be free to go.

So each of the brothers opened up their sacks of grain but when they come to the sack of grain in possession of Benjamin there is the cup, Joseph's silver cup. These men were shocked and stunned to their very core. In agony of heart and soul they all tore their clothing. Tearing clothing was a sign of great distress and grief; it was a sign of mourning. Many years ago the brothers had ripped Joseph's ornate cloak from him and they had dipped it in blood to fool their father. And their father when presented with evidence of the death of Joseph tore his clothing in mourning, now they tear theirs. Now they have no choice but to go back to Joseph's house and to deal with these terrible unexpected events.

CHAPTER THIRTY-ONE

JUDAH

When Judah and his brothers came to Joseph's house, he was still there. They fell before him to the ground. Joseph said to them, "What deed is this that you have done? Do you not know that a man like me can indeed practice divination?" And Judah said, "What shall we say to my lord? What shall we speak? Or how can we clear ourselves? God has found out the guilt of your servants; behold, we are my lord's servants, both we and he also in whose hand the cup has been found." But he said, "Far be it from me that I should do so! Only the man in whose hand the cup was found shall be my servant. But as for you, go up in peace to your father." Then Judah went up to him and said, "Oh, my lord, please let your servant speak a word in my lord's ears, and let not your anger burn against your servant, for you are like Pharaoh himself. My lord asked his servants, saying, 'Have you a father, or a brother?' And we said to my lord, 'We have a father, an old man, and a young brother, the child of his old age. His brother is dead, and he alone is left of his mother's children, and his father loves him.' Then you said to your servants, 'Bring him down to me, that I may set my eyes on him.' We said to my lord, 'The boy cannot leave his father, for if he should leave his father, his father would die.' Then you said to your servants, 'Unless your youngest brother comes down with you, you shall not see my face again.' "When we went back to your servant my father, we told him the words of my lord. And when our father said, 'Go again, buy us a little food,' we said, 'We cannot go down. If our youngest brother goes with us, then we will go down. For we cannot see the man's face unless our youngest brother is with us.' Then your servant my father said to us, 'You know that my wife bore me two sons. One left me, and I said, "Surely he has been torn to pieces," and I have never seen him since. If you take this one also from me, and harm happens to him, you will bring down my gray hairs in evil to Sheol.' "Now therefore, as soon as I come to your servant my father, and the boy is not with us, then, as his life is bound up in the boy's life, as soon as he sees that the boy is not with us, he will die, and your servants will bring down the gray hairs of your servant our father with sorrow to Sheol. For your servant became a pledge of safety for the boy to my father, saying, 'If I do not bring him back to you, then I shall bear the blame before my father all my life.' Now therefore, please let your servant remain instead of the boy as a servant to my lord, and let the boy go back with his brothers. For how can I go back to my father if the boy is not with me? I fear to see the evil that would find my father." (Genesis 44: 14-34)

When we read this passage where Joseph had his confrontation with his brothers regarding the silver cup it was a most incredible, a most powerful moment of high drama and overwhelming emotions.

A reader cannot help but see the tension, drama and poignancy of this moment. Let the reader do this: read aloud Judah's speech contained in Genesis 44:18-34. Read his soliloquy with inflection; read it dramatically as if you were in a play and these were your lines to recite. Imagine the face of Judah, imagine the look in his eyes the body language the use of his hands and arms, and think about all that. Did Judah weep? It would be surprising if he did not.

The brothers all came back to Joseph's house and Joseph was still there. The passage tells us that they fell before him to the ground in a posture of total submission. They knew this man wielded immense power and authority and with a snap of his fingers their life could be forfeit. They were terrified!

Think back if you will back to chapter 37 in Genesis were Joseph had his dreams twenty-two years prior. His brothers were angered by the dreams as we saw and they asked him angry rhetorical question, "Are you indeed to reign over us!?" Yes. Joseph was reigning over them now, yet they do not know that his prophecy has been fulfilled in a most awesome and powerful way.

Joseph continued the drama. He demanded to know what they have done and he challenged them that they surely know he is a man of great power who can practice divination. He was saying that not only does he have great power politically, that he also has great power religiously, that he can see clearly those things that are hidden and oblique.

Judah spoke for the group and he asked essentially, what can we say, what can we do to clear ourselves for we are rightly guilty, God has found out the guilt. Guilt, yes, guilty of terrible cruelty, guilty of selling their brother into slavery and for all they know contributing to his death, guilty of perpetrating a terrible fraud and lie on their father. Ten of the brothers are guilty of all these things and they know it. But they were not guilty of stealing from the Vizier and committing fraud by not paying for the grain. What is interesting here is that Judah consigned the entire group of brothers to share in the judgment against Benjamin. As Benjamin would become a slave, so they will become a slave they will share his accusation, they will share his suffering.

Joseph countered saying that he would not do such a thing but that the person who was guilty, that person would become his slave. Doubtless Joseph had planned this carefully; he had deliberately set out Benjamin to be accused of a crime that he had not committed. How well Joseph knew the agony of such false accusations. Joseph did a hard and difficult thing, but he was for Benjamin and he was seeking to see if he could also still be for his brothers.

Oh there are times in our lives where God engineers very difficult circumstances, very trying circumstances, where as Cowper's hymn says, there is a frowning face of Providence but the smile of God is behind it. What momentarily seems like a horrible affliction bears a glorious fruit of the glory of God.

This is the final test; Joseph will know the true state of the souls of his brothers. Are they truly repentant and sorry for their crime; are they better, wiser more mature men?

Judah makes a very bold move at this point, verbally. He, most likely, moved closer to Joseph and if there were guards there with Joseph we have to wonder if their hands went to their weapons when he moved because what would this man do in such a desperate situation? But Judah began to speak and it is the speech of a broken, repentant and contrite man. Just over two decades prior he had been heartless and callous in devising a scheme to sell his brother for money. But Judah was no longer that man.

Jacob suffered the loss of Joseph for many years. Jacob went without true closure and certainty as to Joseph's fate. There had been no body to bury. And over the years these brothers had seen how their father had grieved and suffered the loss of one that he loved dearly. Perhaps that suffering broke the hard brittle shell of anger and hatred towards Joseph, (and towards Jacob as well) softened their hearts and consciences, made them long for redemption, to right a wrong that they felt they could never change.

The bottom line was whereas they had been all too glad to rid themselves of Joseph then, losing Benjamin now was more than they could bear. Judah could not lose Benjamin; he could not watch his father grieve again for Benjamin as he had for Joseph he could not watch his father die in grief. Judah, himself buried two sons and understood the pain of losing children (Genesis 46:12).

And so Judah did the only thing he knew to do, he began by explaining the situation carefully. He reminded Joseph of the history of the loss of one brother and explained the impact it had on their father. He explained all of this to Joseph as he pled for the freedom of Benjamin. Judah, the principal betrayer of Joseph, through the sacrifice of laying down his own freedom, sought to save Benjamin. He did it for the love of his father. Judah offered to make himself a slave to save Benjamin because he loved his father Jacob. The selfish has become the selfless.

Read it again, the plea of Judah:

"Please, my lord, let your servant say just one word to you. Please, do not be angry with me, even though you are as powerful as Pharaoh himself. "My lord, previously you asked us, your servants, 'Do you have a father or a brother?' And we responded, 'Yes, my lord, we have a father who is an old man, and his youngest son is a child of his old age. His full brother is dead, and he alone is left of his mother's children, and his father loves him very much.' "And you said to us, 'Bring him here so I can see him with my own eyes.' But we said to you, 'My lord, the boy cannot leave his father, for his father would die.' But you told us, 'Unless your youngest brother comes with you, you will never see my face again.' "So we returned to your servant, our father, and told him what you had said. Later, when he said, 'Go back again and buy us more food,' we replied, 'We can't go unless you let our youngest brother go with us. We'll never get to see the man's face unless our youngest brother is with us.' "Then my father said to us, 'As you know, my wife had

two sons, and one of them went away and never returned. Doubtless he was torn to pieces by some wild animal. I have never seen him since. Now if you take his brother away from me, and any harm comes to him, you will send this grieving, white-haired man to his grave.' "And now, my lord, I cannot go back to my father without the boy. Our father's life is bound up in the boy's life. If he sees that the boy is not with us, our father will die. We, your servants, will indeed be responsible for sending that grieving, white-haired man to his grave. My lord, I guaranteed to my father that I would take care of the boy. I told him, 'If I don't bring him back to you, I will bear the blame forever.' "So please, my lord, let me stay here as a slave instead of the boy, and let the boy return with his brothers. For how can I return to my father if the boy is not with me? I couldn't bear to see the anguish this would cause my father!" (Genesis 44: 18-34 NLT)

The transformation of Judah's character, representative of the other nine offending brothers was complete. All those years ago they had acted with what the British legal system terms 'malice aforethought', they had cruelly, out of jealous anger, sold their brother for profit, potentially sending him to his death. They had lied to their father and consigned Jacob to that most agonizing of living emotional wounds, which is the loss of a loved one without closure. Judah, who hatched a scheme to sell Joseph into slavery, would himself become a slave to save his father's beloved son.

In this, Judah acts as a type of Christ, a shadow of gospel story. Judah would give his life, his freedom to redeem the life of Benjamin; he would ransom the youngest brother from slavery as Jesus ransomed us from sin.

In a sense, is a misnomer to refer to the Bible as divided between the Old and the New Testament for the Bible is truly one, long redemption narrative. The early history of the Bible constantly points us to the later times culminating in Christ's saving work. Judah pointed to that Messiah, Jesus who will save his people from sin as Judah would save Benjamin.

Repentance and the willingness to act in repentance; had come to the sons of Jacob.

CHAPTER THIRTY-TWO

TRUE IDENTITY

Then Joseph could not control himself before all those who stood by him. He cried, "Make everyone go out from me." So no one stayed with him when Joseph made himself known to his brothers. And he wept aloud, so that the Egyptians heard it, and the household of Pharaoh heard it. And Joseph said to his brothers, "I am Joseph! Is my father still alive?" But his brothers could not answer him, for they were dismayed at his presence. (Genesis 45:1-3)

One of the archetypes of literature and mythology is that of a child of noble birth, who for safety sake or some other reason hidden among the humble until such a time as they can take their rightful place. In Joseph's case he is a young man born in relative obscurity who comes to a position of great power and authority, not on the basis of his lineage, but on the strength of his character and the abilities that he constantly displayed. Joseph was a slave, who then became a prisoner, who then became the virtual ruler of Egypt.

When the sons of Jacob first laid their eyes on Joseph again, when he was selling grain they, of course, did not know who he was. To them he would have been known by his Egyptian name, Zaphenath-paneah (which, to the best of our knowledge means "God Speaks—He lives").[1] Everything about him would have appeared Egyptian. Men of his station wore gold jewelry and as we have said he would have been completely clean-shaven both face and head. As with other Egyptian men and women, his look would have been somewhat androgynous; he would have worn a wig, his eyes having eye-shadow and eyeliner. His dress would have, most likely, been a fine linen skirt or kilt. His sandals would have been leather. He spoke Egyptian to them and that was interpreted into Hebrew, as we saw earlier. He claimed to have the gift of divination. Nothing would cause them to suspect that he was anyone other than the imperious vizier of Egypt. In demeanor, in appearance and in speech he could not have been more different than his Hebrew family.

Although seemingly, they all had gotten off on the wrong foot when the brothers first came to buy grain, all of that had seemed to be behind them now. It had been explained to them that their previous payment had been returned graciously to them and so that there was no misunderstanding or any ill feeling between they and this Egyptian administrator. The eleven sons had been served a meal in his home and they had spent time talking together. That morning they had left on what seemed to be good terms, but now all of that seems changed and they feel a deep sense of foreboding and danger.

Their brother Judah, who has taken the position as spokesman for them has just finished pleading for the freedom of their youngest brother Benjamin, the one in whose sack of grain that the vizier's cup had been found. Judah had gone so far as to offer himself to be a slave in Benjamin's place.

These eleven sons of Jacob could not believe they could be in any more danger than they were at that moment. However,

---

1   This is the meaning of the names according to the *New American Standard Bible*® (La Habra, CA: The Lockman Foundation, 1995).

ten of the brothers, were about to find out that their worst of all possible nightmares was coming true. They will find themselves standing in the presence of the last person in the world they thought they would ever face.

Up until this time Joseph had restrained himself with tremendous, truly unbelievable, self-control. Oh, he has had his moments when he had to turn away because the emotions were too much but, by and large, Joseph has been able to hold his emotions in check. He could hold his emotions in check no longer.

The agonizing, heartfelt, pleading speech of Judah for the freedom of his youngest brother, Judah's own willingness to take the place of Benjamin lest the suffering kill his father, totally breached Joseph's emotional walls and Joseph could no longer maintain the illusion that he was an Egyptian. He will now show himself to be their Hebrew brother.

Joseph ordered all of his attendants, speaking to them in Egyptian, everyone in the house, except his brothers, to all leave immediately. Joseph began to weep and he wept greatly, he wept with sobs and with tremendous emotion. It is as if a dam had burst in his soul.

When he could, the man spoke to the brothers directly, in Hebrew—their language, not in Egyptian and not through an interpreter as before. He told them, "I am Joseph." then he asked a question, "Is my father still alive?"

"I am Joseph." He could have said, "I am the brother whom you wanted to kill yet I am alive. I am the brother whom you sold into slavery yet I am the second most powerful man in Egypt. I am the brother whom you hated and said that you would never bow to me yet you have bowed to me more than once and I hold the power of life and death over you as we speak! All it would take is a simple phrase and you all, save Benjamin, would die a most agonizing death. I am Joseph!"

But, he did not say that.

Most likely, however, this is exactly what these ten brothers of Joseph were thinking because the Scripture tells us "They could not answer him, for they were dismayed at his presence." Dismayed at his presence—that is probably the grandfather of all understatements. They stared at the face of death, for all they knew. These men were terrified!

CHAPTER THIRTY-THREE

GOD SENT ME

So Joseph said to his brothers, "Come near to me, please." And they came near. And he said, "I am your brother, Joseph, whom you sold into Egypt. And now do not be distressed or angry with yourselves because you sold me here, for God sent me before you to preserve life. For the famine has been in the land these two years, and there are yet five years in which there will be neither plowing nor harvest. And God sent me before you to preserve for you a remnant on earth, and to keep alive for you many survivors. So it was not you who sent me here, but God. He has made me a father to Pharaoh, and lord of all his house and ruler over all the land of Egypt. (Genesis 45:4-8)

Often, when it comes to the Providence of God working in our lives, day in and day out and trusting that Providence is benevolent, is walking by faith and not by sight. Certainly, for long stretches in his life, Joseph had to trust what he could not see. This is an absolutely critical lesson for us, in this life, if we're going to maintain spiritual and emotional balance.

When Joseph was seventeen-years-old, having been sold as

a slave and forcefully marched into Egypt, we could excuse him if he felt totally alone, isolated and forsaken. After all, although Joseph was a man of incredible faith he did not have the advantage of having the testimony of his life, as we do to show how God works. Oh to be sure he had heard how God worked in the life of Abraham, Isaac and his father Jacob but he did not have Romans 8:28.

What Joseph saw through his life from the time of his slavery through the false accusation and imprisonment and into his rise to power was that God was for him. Each time Joseph had a serious life reversal God showed blessings to Joseph and Joseph got the message that although he was in a difficult place he was not in that difficult place alone. God still showed him favor. All of the events, leading up to this moment during his Egyptian sojourn, came together to provide for Joseph a sense of clarity as to the plan and the purpose of God. In short, it all began to make sense.

We must point out again, however, that the clarity of Joseph's life situation is not given to all Christians who suffer trial and affliction in this life. We cannot make the point strongly enough that we, when it comes to God's work in our lives, may have to walk by faith until we see Jesus face to face. The simple fact of the matter is for the Christian we are not called to understand or grasp the reasons of God's providence in our lives but we are called to trust in that providence in our lives. We are called to trust that God is good; that he is for us and that he works all of the events of our lives out for our ultimate good and His own glory. Some events are excruciatingly painful in a variety of ways and faith does not dull that pain. Faith points to the fact that pain and suffering have a purpose.

Joseph acted immediately to calm their fears. He asked his brothers to approach him physically which they did. He did not launch into an angry tirade; he was simply not at that place. He did not demand to know what they were thinking when they betrayed him nor did he seek to heap guilt on them. He did not say these things. Rather Joseph reiterated that he is that Joseph which they sold into slavery in Egypt, however he told them not to be angry with themselves. Joseph said this to his brothers because he has a perspective on what God has been doing in his life and why. Joseph explained to his brothers that he was sent before them by God and he was sent with the purpose to preserve and save their lives.

He explained to them that there are yet five years of famine to be endured and that by his work, they could survive. Joseph told his brothers three separate times that God sent him to Egypt. He told his brothers that God was behind what they did in selling him as a slave. They thought it was their hand that moved against Joseph and in a sense it was but what Joseph could see at this point was there was a larger hand moving the events, a hidden hand that was actually moving these events for Joseph, not against him, and for Joseph's family. In coming to Egypt, Joseph was placed in a position where he could be father to Pharaoh, where he could tend to the needs of Pharaoh, Pharaoh's people and his own.

So for Joseph the issue, primarily, was not his brothers, it was God, all God. God was providentially caring for Abraham's lineage. Matthew Henry wrote,

> Providence looks a great way forward and has a long reach. Even long before the years of plenty, Providence was preparing for the supply of Jacob's house in the years of famine…God often works by contraries. The envy and contention of brethren threaten the ruin of families, yet, in this instance, they prove the occasion of preserving Jacob's family.

Henry goes on to say, "God must have all the glory in the seasonable preservation of his people."[1]

---

1   Matthew Henry, 86.

CHAPTER THIRTY-FOUR

LORD OF ALL EGYPT

*Hurry and go up to my father and say to him, 'Thus says
your son Joseph, God has made me lord of all Egypt. Come
down to me; do not tarry. You shall dwell in the land of
Goshen, and you shall be near me, you and your children
and your children's children, and your flocks, your herds,
and all that you have. There I will provide for you, for there
are yet five years of famine to come, so that you and your
household, and all that you have, do not come to poverty.'
And now your eyes see, and the eyes of my brother Benjamin see, that it is my mouth that speaks to you. You must
tell my father of all my honor in Egypt, and of all that you
have seen. Hurry and bring my father down here." Then he
fell upon his brother Benjamin's neck and wept, and Benjamin wept upon his neck. And he kissed all his brothers
and wept upon them. After that his brothers talked with
him. When the report was heard in Pharaoh's house, "Joseph's brothers have come," it pleased Pharaoh and his servants. And Pharaoh said to Joseph, "Say to your brothers,
'Do this: load your beasts and go back to the land of Canaan, and take your father and your households, and come*

to me, and I will give you the best of the land of Egypt, and you shall eat the fat of the land.' And you, Joseph, are commanded to say, 'Do this: take wagons from the land of Egypt for your little ones and for your wives, and bring your father, and come. Have no concern for your goods, for the best of all the land of Egypt is yours.'" The sons of Israel did so: and Joseph gave them wagons, according to the command of Pharaoh, and gave them provisions for the journey. To each and all of them he gave a change of clothes, but to Benjamin he gave three hundred shekels of silver and five changes of clothes. To his father he sent as follows: ten donkeys loaded with the good things of Egypt, and ten female donkeys loaded with grain, bread, and provision for his father on the journey. Then he sent his brothers away, and as they departed, he said to them, "Do not quarrel on the way." So they went up out of Egypt and came to the land of Canaan to their father Jacob. And they told him, "Joseph is still alive, and he is ruler over all the land of Egypt." And his heart became numb, for he did not believe them. But when they told him all the words of Joseph, which he had said to them, and when he saw the wagons that Joseph had sent to carry him, the spirit of their father Jacob revived. And Israel said, "It is enough; Joseph my son is still alive. I will go and see him before I die." (Genesis 45: 9-28)

Joseph's immediate goal, his immediate action was to take steps to ensure that his father would learn quickly that he Joseph was, in fact, still alive. He wanted his father to know that God has graciously placed him in a position of great authority in Egypt and that Joseph, in that position, could provide for the welfare and the good of his entire family. He wanted them to come down to the land of Goshen where they will be near him. With this he embraced his brother Benjamin and he wept and Benjamin wept with him. And then Joseph kissed his every brother, weeping.

What we see here in the heart of Joseph is a tremendous amount of love for his family, a longing for the family relationship to be restored. He was not using the circumstances as an opportunity for anger, or hatred, or revenge. No, not revenge, but grace, love, mercy, provision and forgiveness.

Pharaoh heard of these events and it pleased him that Joseph was in the process of reunification with his family. Out of gratitude for all of the hard work of Joseph and how Joseph had in many ways literally saved his country Pharaoh extended blessings and provision to Joseph's family. Transportation was made available in the form of wagons to transport Jacob and his household to Egypt; all that they need will be provided. The sons of Jacob were provided with new clothing, Benjamin receiving the greatest blessing. Joseph sent his father donkeys loaded with the goods of Egypt, with grain and bread and all that is needed for the journey. But before they go Joseph said to his brothers, "Do not quarrel on the way."

Why did Joseph instruct his brothers not to quarrel with each other? Well, after all, these were his brothers and he knew them well; he knew their proclivities and the dynamics of their relationships. Joseph wanted his brothers to do the work necessary to place these events in the past. Joseph wanted to look forward, to a time of blessing and joy. He did not want discord over events that cannot be changed.

So the sons of Jacob journey back to Canaan to retrieve their father and return to Egypt. When they see their father they tell him that Joseph is still alive and that he is ruler over all the land of Egypt. We read that Jacob's heart became numb; this incredibly wonderful news staggered Jacob, so much so that a literal reading of the Hebrew indicates he almost fainted. Who can blame Jacob? These were words that Jacob thought he would never hear.

His beloved son Joseph is alive!

It is almost too good to be true. Reading in between the lines it is almost as if Jacob's mind fights against this new present reality that he has been informed of.

However, when the brothers persisted in their report and when Jacob saw the wagons and the donkeys all laden with provisions and goods of Egypt then the reality, this new joyous reality took hold in the heart of this aged man.

Joseph is alive!

"And Israel said, 'It is enough; Joseph my son is still alive. I will go and see him before I die.' "

CHAPTER THIRTY-FIVE

DETOUR TO EGYPT

So Israel took his journey with all that he had and came to Beersheba, and offered sacrifices to the God of his father Isaac. And God spoke to Israel in visions of the night and said, "Jacob, Jacob." And he said, "Here I am." Then he said, "I am God, the God of your father. Do not be afraid to go down to Egypt, for there I will make you into a great nation. I myself will go down with you to Egypt, and I will also bring you up again, and Joseph's hand shall close your eyes." Then Jacob set out from Beersheba. The sons of Israel carried Jacob their father, their little ones, and their wives, in the wagons that Pharaoh had sent to carry him. They also took their livestock and their goods, which they had gained in the land of Canaan, and came into Egypt, Jacob and all his offspring with him, 7 his sons, and his sons' sons with him, his daughters, and his sons' daughters. All his offspring he brought with him into Egypt... All the persons belonging to Jacob who came into Egypt, who were his own descendants, not including Jacob's sons' wives, were sixty-six persons in all. And the sons of Joseph, who were born to him in Egypt, were two. All the persons of the house

171

of Jacob who came into Egypt were seventy. He had sent Judah ahead of him to Joseph to show the way before him in Goshen, and they came into the land of Goshen. Then Joseph prepared his chariot and went up to meet Israel his father in Goshen. He presented himself to him and fell on his neck and wept on his neck a good while. Israel said to Joseph, "Now let me die, since I have seen your face and know that you are still alive." Joseph said to his brothers and to his father's household, "I will go up and tell Pharaoh and will say to him, 'My brothers and my father's household, who were in the land of Canaan, have come to me. And the men are shepherds, for they have been keepers of livestock, and they have brought their flocks and their herds and all that they have.' When Pharaoh calls you and says, 'What is your occupation?' you shall say, 'Your servants have been keepers of livestock from our youth even until now, both we and our fathers,' in order that you may dwell in the land of Goshen, for every shepherd is an abomination to the Egyptians."… Thus Israel settled in the land of Egypt, in the land of Goshen. And they gained possessions in it, and were fruitful and multiplied greatly. And Jacob lived in the land of Egypt seventeen years. So the days of Jacob, the years of his life, were 147 years. (Genesis 46:1-7; 26-34; Genesis 47:27-28)

Jacob, also called Israel, left Canaan with his family. Canaan, the land promised to his grandfather and his father; the land of promise and covenant. God came to Jacob in a vision of the night to assuage any concerns he had about leaving this Promised Land to go down to Egypt. Jacob was promised that even as he goes down into Egypt with his great family that God will be with him that he will make him a mighty nation and return his people back to the land of promise. God also graciously promised Jacob that his beloved son Joseph will close his eyes when he dies.

Jacob was initially concerned that he was taking a detour on his road to the fulfillment of God's promises to his family. It seemed a divergence from the planned pathway. In the journey of our lives God almost never seems to take us directly from point A to point B. To utilize a metaphor, God seems to take us off of the interstate highway and has us continue our journey on back roads by a seemingly circuitous route. Our heavenly father has a destination in mind for us, for our lives, he has a direction and a place that he is taking us toward. We are so often in a big hurry about our lives, but God is not in a big hurry. His concern is not with the speed of our travel, His concern is that we are prepared properly in spiritual growth and maturity for the destination that he wants to bring us to.

God has his purposes in this four hundred year divergence of the Hebrew people from the Promised Land. This interlude is not without good reasons. God was fully at work in the Egyptian sojourn of Jacob's people just as much as he was in Joseph's journey to Egypt wearing the chains of slavery. What we truly need to grasp in all of this is that the whole idea of a divergence in our lives is really a misnomer. We see it as a delay or perhaps a halting in the work that God has called us to do but that is not the case, we are where we are meant to be. What we call divergence is not an accident but an integral part in His plan for our lives.

In the economy of God in our lives, divergent times have their purpose and their blessing. We may not be the object of that blessing. Perhaps we could look at the life of John Newton as an example of this concept. Newton was blessed with a mother who was a very godly woman who prayed over him and taught him in the things of God. She laid a foundation in his soul but when she died while Newton was still a boy it broke his heart and turned him against the God of his mother. He grew into a wild youth and a wild young man. Ultimately Newton became a slave trader. Though for a time Newton was done with God, God was not done with Newton. Over a period of years the spirit of God moved in the life of John Newton and brought him to true faith and repentance. Newton became a mighty preacher and a prolific hymn writer.

John Newton is perhaps most noted for his writing that most beloved of hymns, "Amazing Grace." Although Newton wrote the lyrics the music, strictly speaking, the melody, was not his own. The melody was inspired by African mourning chants sung by the Africans as they lay chained in Newton's slave ship to their final destination. It was the mournful, soulful singing of these men, women and children that became the foundation for the music of this most powerful hymn. Without the divergence in the life of John Newton, without his hearing these African melodies and without the movement of the Holy Spirit that brought him to faith and repentance, anchoring him to a bedrock truth that God's grace was truly amazing, without all of this, we would not have this music. This divergence had a purpose; God was in it.

God makes us into what He would have us be in the divergences of our lives.

So the house of Jacob, all seventy of them, caravanned to Egypt and Joseph rode his chariot to reunite with his father. We read that Joseph embraced his father, that he fell on his neck and he wept a long time. What a wonderful, blessed and poignant scene.

Joseph explained to his family that he will go to Pharaoh and advise that his family are keepers of livestock. Joseph coached them that at some point in the future when they have an audience with Pharaoh that they are to reiterate this truth that they are shepherds. The Scripture then proceeds to tell us that shepherds are an abomination to the Egyptians.

How is this helpful? Well, it is a further movement of the hand of God and provision for the descendants of Abraham. There were two issues that the children of Israel faced as they settled in the land of Egypt. One issue was being an encroachment on their property by native Egyptians. This was an ongoing issue in the land of Canaan. Since shepherds are an abomination to the Egyptians the likelihood was increased that they and their land will be given a wide berth by the Egyptians. Also, Jacob wanted to keep his descendents Hebrew. He did not want them assimilated into the Egyptian culture or the Egyptian religions. Joseph out of necessity had been pulled into the Egyptian culture but not the religion. He still worshiped the one true God. But doubtless the social pressures on Joseph to fully assimilate were tremendous and a lesser person might cave in to the pressure. Moses will make very clear to the children of Israel centuries later that they are a special and a unique people.[1] Moses also made the point strongly that God wanted Israel to maintain its own religious and ethnic identity. Adopting the religion of surrounding nations, marrying into the societies would ultimately compromise their faith. Having a separate area or region in the nation of Egypt would assist greatly in keeping that separate identity.

God was gracious to Jacob and gave him seventeen more years of life. During this time the family of Jacob increased both in wealth and in size. Of great blessing as well was that Jacob had a number of years to be with his beloved son Joseph. Doubtless these were blessed years for both Joseph and his father. Before he left Egypt Jacob had told his sons that he was ready to die knowing that his son Joseph lived. Grace and mercy give him additional years, almost as many years with Joseph again as they were apart. And then the time will come when Jacob in the moving prose of Scripture "breathed his last and was gathered to his people."[2]

---

1   Deuteronomy 7:6
2   Genesis 49:33

CHAPTER THIRTY-SIX

GOOD PURPOSES

When Joseph's brothers saw that their father was dead, they said, "It may be that Joseph will hate us and pay us back for all the evil that we did to him." So they sent a message to Joseph, saying, "Your father gave this command before he died: 'Say to Joseph, "Please forgive the transgression of your brothers and their sin, because they did evil to you."' And now, please forgive the transgression of the servants of the God of your father." Joseph wept when they spoke to him. His brothers also came and fell down before him and said, "Behold, we are your servants." But Joseph said to them, "Do not fear, for am I in the place of God? As for you, you meant evil against me, but God meant it for good, to bring it about that many people should be kept alive, as they are today. So do not fear; I will provide for you and your little ones." Thus he comforted them and spoke kindly to them. So Joseph remained in Egypt, he and his father's house. Joseph lived 110 years. And Joseph saw Ephraim's children of the third generation. The children also of Machir the son of Manasseh were counted as Joseph's own. And Joseph said to his brothers, "I am about to die, but God will

visit you and bring you up out of this land to the land that
he swore to Abraham, to Isaac, and to Jacob." Then Joseph
made the sons of Israel swear, saying, "God will surely visit
you, and you shall carry up my bones from here." So Joseph
died, being 110 years old. They embalmed him, and he was
put in a coffin in Egypt. (Genesis 50: 15-26)

When I set out to write this book, a key point occurred to me to elaborate on, being that suffering comes to us from different angles in this life and different directions and sources, some of which are from people and some from life itself.

Two examples of this happened during the writing with tragedies that occurred here in the United States within weeks of one another. On the afternoon on May 20, 2013 an F-five tornado ripped through the town of Moore Oklahoma killing over twenty people and injuring almost four hundred. The awful tragedy was that the storm obliterated an elementary school and seven children died. Suffering comes to us simply from living on this planet where there are weather extremes and other events such as floods and earthquakes, what we call natural disasters. Of course there are terrible accidents that are fatal, a seeming concurrence of events that are deadly.

Yet there are those tragedies that are acts of malice, of evil. An example of this is the Boston Marathon bombing which took place less than six weeks prior to the Moore Tornado, on April 15, 2013. This was terroristic murder plain and simple, the act of two young men moved by religious extremism to murder non-adherents to Islam. This was a deliberate act where the Tsarnaev brothers built devices to maim and kill as many as possible. Three died and over two hundred fifty were injured. The suffering and death resulted from a-moral choice that murder of civilians was acceptable. There was no moral choice involved in the Moore Oklahoma tornado and that is the primary difference. Suffering comes in the form of disaster beyond our reach or it comes from a moral (or immoral) choice of an individual or individuals. To state the obvious, our moral and immoral choices are not made in a vacuum, but rather have profound impact on others. The profound impact of moral choices has been a key component of the Joseph narrative.

There is evil in this world and that evil is on full display daily. The most casual reading of the daily news should make clear the existence and prevalence of evil around us. Evil impacts our lives. One of the most pernicious aspects of the prosperity gospel is the idea that being in the center of the will of God will build a hedge around us and guarantee our physical and emotional safety. That is total and utter nonsense as we will see as we read the book of Acts in the New Testament as well as the letters by Paul, James, Peter, and John. Christians suffer in this world at the hands of others. Christians are persecuted, attacked and killed.

After Jacob died and was buried events transpired that are both sad and terribly human. These ten sons of Jacob send word to Joseph that their father's final wish is that he, Joseph, would forgive them for their transgression against him.

Joseph wept when he heard this. It must have broken his heart to think that at long last and after everything, that his brothers still did not trust his good character and his good will toward them. Apparently, these brothers thought that mercy was extended to them primarily to benefit their father and their participation is incidental. Nearly forty years have passed since the events of that day at that dry cistern when they acted so maliciously to Joseph. At that time, malice had been such a major part of their character that it was difficult for them now to see that malice was not in the character of their brother Joseph. They tended to think that he would treat them as they had treated Joseph. His heart is in a different place.

Joseph spoke to his brothers directly and he told them essentially three things: first he told them not to fear and not be afraid of him. Second, he made a statement through a rhetorical question: "Am I in the place of God?" Thirdly brothers, that what you did, you meant with evil intentions, you meant it for evil against me, but God meant it for good, to save many people.

In a following chapter we will examine the issue of forgiveness. But for now we want to consider the entire issue in Joseph's life in the purpose and context of the work of God. We will, at best, scratch the surface on the whole matter.

What leaps off the page at us is that Joseph had a very clear sense of God's purposes in his ordeal, in his suffering at the hands of his brothers, of Potiphar's wife and of the neglect of the cupbearer. Joseph did not gloss over or make light of the evil done to him. No, he did not soft-pedal the issue; he called their actions what they were, he called them evil.

Joseph knew that God had used him as an instrument of preservation for his family and for the nation of Egypt. Joseph knew that the actions of his brothers help to set all of these events in motion that Joseph played a part in. In short Joseph saw in all of these events the larger, hidden, invisible hand of God. Joseph was able to see in his life the practical reality of Romans 8:28, that, in fact, all things do indeed work toward the good for God's people. Not all events are good in and of themselves but the sum of all events, good and bad, take us heavenward, bring us closer to God and His purposes.

He was granted the discernment to see God in all his life events. Joseph could see where the invisible hand moved in events we humanly call reversals as well as the triumphs. By the time he was thirty, Joseph had spent almost half of his life in servitude. His dreams of greatness at age seventeen were deferred for many years. Gary Thomas writes,

> God's blessings do not always come with the speed of a bullet but rather the slow pace of a glacier... One thing is clear: God won't be rushed. Without a willingness to wait we will be frequently frustrated with God and may become disillusioned with our faith.... God never promises that our present circumstances will always make sense. Sometimes the present will have to become the past be-

fore what we're going through can become even remotely understandable…. God is not merely concerned with results, but also with character-and few things produce character like a learning to wait…."

He goes on to say, "Maturity in the faith is no guarantee that we will experience less suffering. In fact, it well may mean we will experience more."[1]

Thomas goes on to mention Teresa of Avilla, who suffered from migraines, Brother Lawrence, who suffered with gout and Richard Baxter who suffered with cancer. Suffering is not the bane of our existence, a pain to be avoided, but rather is the hammer and chisel in the hand of God to shape us into the image of His son. It is only in suffering that we begin to move toward mature faith.

He, who sets the boundaries of our afflictions, applies them with the same wisdom and insight He used to create the universe. We can rest in the fact that even when we are in the midst of the most severe storm of suffering, we are still in the hollow of His hand. Joseph was always safe in the hollow of God's hand.

To bring about Christ's character in us, God will take from our grasp what we would otherwise hold on to, that we might hold onto Jesus. Our character, not our comfort, is of paramount importance to God. "Trust and obey," as the old hymn says,"… for there's no other way to be happy in Jesus than to trust and obey." Purpose, there is always a purpose, as our suffering is not random.

As Jerry Bridges says,

…but, note also, the twofold objective of God's providence: His own glory and the good of his people. These two objectives are never antithetical; they are always in harmony with each other. God never pursues his glory at

---

1   Gary Thomas, *Authentic Faith* (Grand Rapids: Zondervan, 2002), 44, 63.

the expense of the good of his people, nor does he ever seek our good at the expense of his glory. He has designed his eternal purpose so that his glory... .[2]

What this meant for Joseph is that the difficult and hard events in his life were not only for God's glory but also ultimately for his good. Joseph benefited spiritually from the events of his life. This is important for us to realize, because we must see ourselves not as merely cogs in the great machinery of God, we must also see ourselves as objects of His love and care. While all things ultimately are for His glory, we must always keep sight of the fact that the very hairs on our heads are numbered. We must remember the lessons of Psalm 139, that God knows intimately everything about us and is involved in all the moments and minutes of our lives. As we said at the beginning of this book we are not deists. When Joseph was betrayed by his brothers, God was there. When Joseph was forcibly taken to Egypt, God was there. When Joseph was put on the auction block, sold like a piece of cattle, God was there. God was there when he was in the household of Potiphar, and he saw when young Joseph was sorely tempted and resisted temptation that he might not dishonor God. God was there when Joseph was thrown into prison unjustly. God was there when Joseph was forgotten for another two years in prison. God was there when Joseph was brought before Pharaoh and then made the second most powerful man in the world. In all of these events God was there in the life of Joseph, working out for his own divine glory and also for the good of Joseph to make him a good, just, kind, patient man. He was made first and foremost humble, that God might use him greatly.

God developed Joseph's true character over time; character is never an overnight event. Our character is developed through what the Bible calls 'chastisement'. For us the word lends itself to a negative connotation, that of punishment.

---

2   Jerry Bridges, *Trusting God Even When Life Hurt* (Colorado Springs, CO: NavPress, 2008), 35.

Divine chastisement here though is not so much a re-buke for wrong doing, but a loving father's training and education of his own children whom he dearly loves and for whom he desires the very best. Suffering then is the Christian's training ground. It shows that God has not finished with us, but is refining and polishing us. On this training ground we are made more prayerful and depen-dent upon God. On this training ground we learn more of God's total sufficiency for our insufficiency. On this training ground we learn valuable lessons in humility and Christian sympathy. This training ground painfully prunes us so that we can bear more fruit to God's glory (John 15:2), weaning us away from the trivial things of time which can so engross us, and drawing us that much more closer to God and the promises of His Word. In a nutshell, the training ground of divine chastisement makes us more like the Saviour Who first loved us.[3]

---

3   Timothy Cross, "Divine Chastisement: Blessed are the Buffeted" (online at Earthen Vessel Journal: http://www.earthenvesseljournal. com, 2013)

CHAPTER THIRTY-SEVEN

FORGIVENESS

Forgiveness can be the most difficult of human endeavors. On the face of it, we seem hard-wired for many actions and behaviors such as the drive for sexuality and self-protection. Forgiveness, however, is not a default position; it is not hardwired into our psyche. Forgiveness is a spark of the divine, a glance heavenward, homeward and a reminder of an existence beyond our current sight.

Forgiveness brings us home ultimately; it is the end of the prodigal's journey. God's forgiveness of our sins facilitates the restoral and renewal of our relationship with Him as a human race. Forgiveness and Grace are completely intertwined and co-joined. Relationships, in the long-term cannot exist without forgiveness; it is the critical lubricant for relationships between individuals and with society around us. Without forgiveness, Joseph could not have reconciled with his family. Just as the issue of forgiveness confronted Joseph, so it confronts us all in this day and time.

At this point it is important to hone our definition of *Forgiveness*, what it is, what it is not. We will start with the negative, with what Forgiveness is not.

- Forgiveness is not releasing someone from facing the legal or logical consequences of their action. Actions that require forgiveness often involve, by their scope, the intervention of society and the legal system. This writer once had a loaded revolver stuck in his face by a bank-robber. Forgiveness may be given for the trauma of having a deadly weapon used against you (or the implied threat of the weapon) but the bank-robber still spent time in jail.
- Forgiveness does not forestall justice; God is just and justice is vital for any society for the society to survive.
- Forgiveness and revenge are totally incompatible.
- Forgiveness does not result, necessarily, in restored trust or a restored relationship. A betrayed spouse is well within their rights to require proof of changed behavior and fidelity. If a person has endured emotional or physical abuse they do well to determine if there has, in fact, been a true change in behavior. Forgiveness does not mean we divest ourselves of common sense and become gullible.

So this raises the question as to what forgiveness is.

Some time back this writer conducted an informal poll among several friends and colleagues to get their perspectives and opinions on a definition of forgiveness, so something of a virtual roundtable was created to pick each other's brains. To sum up the results we make the following points:

- Forgiveness relinquishes the right or desire to personally punish the offender.
- Forgiveness refuses to let past wounds control you.
- Forgiveness can encompass self protection, the careful setting of boundaries going forward.
- God's love and forgiveness of us motivate us to forgive others.
- Forgiveness is love, motivated by God and forgiveness is a form of suffering for God.

So we see that forgiveness is both complex and simple: complex due to the complexity of relationships and their variations, as simple as injustice that cuts across the board. What was very clear from the survey responses was that forgiveness and forgetting do not equate, a point we hinted at earlier. By that we mean that forgiveness and forgetting are God actions. For us forgiveness does not equate to forgetting the offense; wisdom dictates to remember it.

What do we mean by that? What we mean is that if God is offended and forgives He is, after all, divine; He has the option to forget. Our offense against him places Him in no danger. However the offense of another against us may place us in grave earthly danger. Our current level of existence is on a completely different plane and we are both divine and human, a hybrid. The need for self-protection does not hold the same imperative for God as it does for us.

Some people may commit an offense against us and we choose to relinquish any right to repay them for their action ourselves. And the key is 'ourselves' but we may wisely choose to protect ourselves against them offending us further and we may choose to allow them to face the legal consequences of any action that is illegal itself. To expound further on some earlier examples, if a person robs me by gunpoint, I may choose to forgive them the offense and not hold it against them personally or seek to retaliate myself but that does not mean that I do not have the right to involve law-enforcement and see them face legal consequences for their illegal act.

Another example might be a woman who in a marriage relationship has been physically abused by her husband. There may be forgiveness of the action, no desire for personal revenge but the spouse may very well face the legal consequences. The woman to protect herself and any children involved may terminate the marriage. Forgiveness is not exclusive of protecting ourselves from further harm. We do not relinquish the right of self-defense.

Joseph's actions toward his brothers when he first saw them after a twenty-two year absence were reasonable actions of self defense and self protection. Certainly Joseph was not in any

physical danger from his brothers, as we have said. Joseph, however, placed himself in a position where he could minimize any
emotional pain, any further trauma from his brother's actions.
By this we're saying again that forgiveness is not synonymous
with reconciliation. Forgiveness may very well offer reconciliation but the realization must be made that reconciliation involves
more than one person. For Joseph and his brothers to reconcile
meant his brothers needed to show that they were changed men,
that they were no longer a danger to Joseph emotionally nor a
danger to Benjamin physically. As we saw in our text Joseph
was willing to reconcile but he took steps to make sure that his
brothers were ready to reconcile as well.

Are there limitations on forgiveness? In other words, are we
given an option where we can set a certain number of infractions,
a particular number of offenses and then, when that threshold is
passed, forgive no more? If the brothers of Joseph had engaged
in further deception or betrayal could he then declare that his
reserves of forgiveness were depleted? If we are honest with ourselves, perhaps we do wonder if, in fact, forgiveness has boundaries.

In Matthew's gospel this is loosely the scenario that drives
the question that Peter posed to Jesus about the limits of forgiveness. Religious leaders in Israel taught that forgiveness was
only to be extended three times but on a fourth similar offense,
all bets were off. Peter, evidently felt that by showing forgiveness
beyond the prescribed current religious thought he was being
generous, magnanimous.

Jesus addressed Peter's potential limitations this way in Matthew:

> Then Peter came up and said to him, "Lord, how often will
> my brother sin against me, and I forgive him? As many as
> seven times?" Jesus said to him, "I do not say to you seven
> times, but seventy-seven times. "Therefore the kingdom of
> heaven may be compared to a king who wished to settle

accounts with his servants. When he began to settle, one was brought to him who owed him ten thousand talents. And since he could not pay, his master ordered him to be sold, with his wife and children and all that he had, and payment to be made. So the servant fell on his knees, imploring him, 'Have patience with me, and I will pay you everything.' And out of pity for him, the master of that servant released him and forgave him the debt. But when that same servant went out, he found one of his fellow servants who owed him a hundred denarii, and seizing him, he began to choke him, saying, 'Pay what you owe.' So his fellow servant fell down and pleaded with him, 'Have patience with me, and I will pay you.' He refused and went and put him in prison until he should pay the debt. When his fellow servants saw what had taken place, they were greatly distressed, and they went and reported to their master all that had taken place. Then his master summoned him and said to him, 'You wicked servant! I forgave you all that debt because you pleaded with me. And should not you have had mercy on your fellow servant, as I had mercy on you?' And in anger his master delivered him to the jailers, until he should pay all his debt. So also my heavenly Father will do to every one of you, if you do not forgive your brother from your heart." (Matthew 18:22-35)

We notice one point that is made indirectly in Jesus' parable: the severity of the offense is detailed yet there is no idea of "… this offense is too great and hence unforgivable." Jesus does not provide a series of loopholes to be applied to his command. In other words, for the Christian, forgiveness is not optional; we are not given a choice as to whether we will, or will not forgive. We are not provided with a short list of unforgiveable acts. Forgiveness is not like coupons in a coupon book where they are used up; rather the implication is that the supply of forgiveness is limitless.

That forgiveness is not optional does not lessen the difficulty and arduousness often involved in obeying Jesus' directive. That is not lost on our Lord, for he knows personally the weight of the demand. Remember, Jesus was scourged and crucified, a most heinous, brutal and cruel death.

We read from the prophet Isaiah:

> *He was despised and rejected by men; a man of sorrows, and acquainted with grief; and as one from whom men hide their faces he was despised, and we esteemed him not. Surely he has borne our griefs and carried our sorrows; yet we esteemed him stricken, smitten by God, and afflicted. But he was pierced for our transgressions; he was crushed for our iniquities; upon him was the chastisement that brought us peace, and with his wounds we are healed. All we like sheep have gone astray; we have turned—every one—to his own way; and the LORD has laid on him the iniquity of us all. Yet it was the will of the LORD to crush him; he has put him to grief; when his soul makes an offering for guilt, he shall see his offspring; he shall prolong his days; the will of the LORD shall prosper in his hand. Out of the anguish of his soul he shall see and be satisfied; by his knowledge shall the righteous one, my servant, make many to be accounted righteous, and he shall bear their iniquities. Therefore I will divide him a portion with the many, and he shall divide the spoil with the strong, because he poured out his soul to death and was numbered with the transgressors; yet he bore the sin of many, and makes intercession for the transgressors. (Isaiah 53:4-12)*

The suffering Isaiah so descriptively foretold and the gospels recounted made the contrast of the terrible suffering and the astounding forgiveness all the more stark and powerful. Jesus, his skin shredded by a flogging, his body pierced by spikes, forgave his assailants from the cross. He had every right to be angry at his totally undeserved treatment. Not only did Jesus have the right,

He had the authority to stop it all and level judgment on his tor-
mentors. He had legions of angelic beings at his disposal to free
him and visit wrath on the ones who crucified Him. But Jesus
chose to stay, and to die for our sins. So when we are mistreated,
our calling is to follow in the footsteps of our older brother Jesus,
and to forgive. Sometimes are called to endure what is humanly
unendurable.

So we forgive. We forgive because it is a command, a requirement of our faith that we can neither get around nor ignore. Why
would God place this stipulation out there as critical to our faith,
our relationship with Him? Forgiveness is for some, the hardest
most taxing struggle of their lives. It is easy to declare fearlessly
this biblical truth but we need to honest about the price involved
for some people who have suffered terribly at the hands of another. The hard evil hands of humans steal, abuse, enslave and
murder other human beings; indeed the list of offenses is legion.
Honestly, it can be easy to demand of another, a specific action
we ourselves have never had to do. So while we cannot negate the
clear directive of scripture we do well to remember that others
may suffer in ways we can scarcely imagine.

Forgiveness is possible, even in the most extreme of circumstances.

In her book, *The Devil in Pew Number Seven*, Rebecca Nichols Alonzo told the story of a childhood marked by terror at the
hands of a disgruntled man in her father's church. The man,
Horry James Watts, a local businessman, resented some of the
decisions made by the new pastor, Rebecca's father, and began a
reign of terror to force the pastor to resign his position and leave.
This would allow Watts, once again, to control the church. First
there were hang up calls to the parsonage phone and then there
were threats. The threats escalated to dynamite blasts in the front
yard of the pastor's home.

For all of this Pastor Robert Nichols, and his wife Ramona,
would not leave. They were doing God's work in this little church.
Lives were touched and changed and they believed it was imper-

ative to endure the persecution for their Lord's sake. Rather than strike out, they prayed for Horry Watts, that he would see his sin and repent. They prayed to forgive this man who harassed them for five years and through their actions and words, taught their children that forgiveness was the only Christian response. But it did not, in human terms, end well.

The Nichols offered shelter into their home to a woman caught in an abusive relationship. Mr. Watts goaded the estranged husband into violent action and the man came to the Nichols home where he shot and seriously wounded Pastor Nichols and then murdered his wife, Ramona Nichols. Pastor Nichols, a broken man, died a few years later. Years afterward, Mr. Watts finally faced justice and jail for his actions.

Although Rebecca's parents were gone, God had placed a good and wise aunt into her life who adopted her and her brother. This aunt provided love and stability for these two emotionally wounded children.

Ten years after the death of her mother, Horry Watts called to speak with Rebecca on the phone. It was not a lengthy conversation. The tormentor and driving force behind the death of her parents asked for her forgiveness for all the terrible things he had done. With that said, he broke down in tears. In spite of his hatred and malice, Watt's evil could not cover over and eradicate the kindness and Christian character of the Nichols. In the end, love and forgiveness won. Watts, while in prison, alone with the consequences of his evil, came to true faith and repentance. He wanted to publically offer restitution to the children. Rebecca Nichols forgave Horry James Watts because Christ requires forgiveness of us.

Jesus called us to love and pray for those who persecute us for our faith and consider us an enemy. This was the choice of the Nichols family with Horry Watts. Joseph would not be whole if he didn't forgive those who wronged him.

We are also to forgive those who mistreat us for reasons more personal than religious, of malice, hatred or indifference. Often the need for forgiveness arises not from a major event or two but from a series of infractions over a lengthy time period. The issue may not be the white hot anger of a major dispute but the petty sufferings that pile up into a mountain of bitterness and resentment. Frankly, this was in large part, in the mind of Joseph's brothers, their goad. They were angry over the combination of the favoritism expressed in clothing and Joseph's dreams. This is a scenario for spouses, family and colleagues, this build-up over time of smaller incidents that fester.

Forgiveness is a moral choice. That people may choose to forgive, or not, gives rise to different scenarios. A person may choose to harden their heart towards another. A person may grasp the reigns of their own soul and decide towards refusal and anger. Such a position is fraught with emotional and spiritual peril. Jesus addressed the unwillingness to forgive without equivocation.

> For if you forgive others their trespasses, your heavenly Father will also forgive you, but if you do not forgive others their trespasses, neither will your Father forgive your trespasses. (Matthew 6:14, 15)

> And whenever you stand praying, forgive, if you have anything against anyone, so that your Father also who is in heaven may forgive you your trespasses." (Mark 11:25)

We as Christians must forgive those who sin against us. If, in the final analysis, we are unwilling to forgive it calls our salvation into question. Jesus is not addressing the severity of the insult or the transgression rather He is simply stating the necessity, the requirements placed upon all of us who follow Him. That is not to say that it is easy and that forgiveness is without cost.

We forgive and we acknowledge that forgiveness is a divine action. Forgiveness originates with God. That is to say that God started the entire process of forgiveness. Jesus going to the cross

is the apex of God's forgiving action. God in the cross was doing the work necessary; after all we are transgressors, we have
broken God's laws and we have offended his righteousness with
our unrighteousness. Our rebellious sin, our self will and desire
to rule over ourselves is an affront to the goodness of God and
the goodness of his character. We need forgiving because the
Scripture tells us clearly we are all sinners and the wages, the just
deserving of that sin, is our death. Indeed, apart from Christ, we
are dead already.

We must see ourselves all as sinners deserving the wrath of
God. This requires honest self-assessment and insight to see our
culpability, as God sees it. We forgive because we were and are
forgiven sinners ourselves. The parable of the unforgiving servant found in Matthew 18 highlights our problem when we do
not properly see our own sin. If we justify our own behavior and
see ourselves self righteously it is easy to hang onto a vengeful,
unforgiving spirit. Please do not confuse the inability or unwillingness to forgive with a proper assessment of sinful action. It is
one thing for a person robbed to honestly declare the perpetrator
a thief; it is another matter for the victim to take it out on the
thief's hide. When we see ourselves correctly as sinners deserving judgment we are compelled to forgive. If we deem another's
offense unforgivable, we're saying our sins, in comparison, are
not that bad really.

Denying forgiveness, at its core, is a dishonest act. An unforgiving person makes themselves their own god and crowns
themselves as righteous and above reproach. They, perhaps unwittingly, declare themselves as above the sins of others. The
only person who could ever rightly take that position of God-
equal personal righteousness, Jesus, forgave others their offense
against himself.

As much as anything, the real point of the parable that Jesus
tells in Matthew 18 is self-honesty. We ourselves must see our
sin and our sin-debt honestly and correctly. Part of our sinful
tendency is to minimize or hide our own sins and highlight and

maximize the sins of others. This is precisely the issue that be-devils many marriages and families. We can not be so proud (and pride really is the beginning of the matter) to minimize our own responsibility and maximize the responsibility of others; we are not allowed that privilege. No, rather, God wants us to understand that when it comes to transgressions and sins against another that He, God is the one who must be answered to. In other words God firmly maintains His right to be the judge, the dispenser of justice. He does not give that right to us. When we refuse to forgive others who have sinned against us and do not recognize that the ultimate sin is not against us but it is against God and his authority. We are trying to take over God's position as the rightful judge ourselves. Yes, we are offended against. Others do hurt us and sometimes grievously. People do terrible, awful things to other human beings. What this parable is teaching us is that our offenses against the good and righteous judge, God, is infinitely greater than all of our offenses against others. If the righteous judge forgives us sins committed against himself as we saw in Matthew, we are to do the same.

When a person endures a terrible emotional trauma, as Joseph did, they may have to work through the stages of grief (Denial, Anger, Bargaining, Depression and Acceptance), especially anger-to arrive at a place of forgiveness. For many of us working through anger is often a process that involves time.

That processing time can last years. A passage of years can provide perspective on the offense and facilitate a more measured response. The passage of time was important to season and mature Joseph, to dim some of the pain and stave off emotions of anger. Anger must be processed. When a person is violated they may experience great, almost overwhelming anger. We, as believers, want to respond Christianly when angered; we want to be angry and sin not and not let the sun go down on our wrath.

The end of the matter was Joseph's acceptance. Acceptance implies a cessation of the struggle-no more fighting-stillness. It is being still. Being still is the thrust of Psalms 46:10; it is knowing that God is God, supreme, infinitely wise. This is tied to trusting God even though his purposes are, at the moment, inscrutable.

Stillness is not resignation. Rather, stillness trusts that in the given situation and circumstances God is very active and involved. He is not still; he is actively working on our behalf. Most often, we see, not the direct hand of God but rather we see after the fact where his hand has already been, as Joseph saw.

Joseph saw the good hand of God, even in his suffering and he showed a great magnanimous character in forgiving his brothers. Behind his magnanimous spirit was honesty, humility, self-integrity and spiritual depth. When their father, Jacob, died, the ten offending brothers, fearing reprisal sought to stay Joseph's vengeful hand. But Joseph's hand was not vengeful. Joseph wept when they came begging for forgiveness through an intermediary (See the narrative in Genesis 50). He asked, "...am I in the place of God?" As much as he had been wronged by his brothers, Joseph knew it was not his place to act and judge over his brothers. His response was not one of anger but one of kindness and grace. Joseph was far larger, a far greater person than them. He had largeness of character.

In his great novel, *The Pillars of the Earth*, Ken Follett masterfully creates a story of the building of a great medieval cathedral. A main character in the story is the Prior of Kingsbridge (the fictional town) Phillip. Phillip desires to build a great church for the glory of God. To do so he will battle a bishop, the aristocracy and the elements. Not the least of his struggles is with a sub-prior who is jealous of Phillip's influence and position, Remigius. Remigius is small, petty, and mean, and works constantly to undermine Phillip in the hope of becoming prior himself.

After years of underhanded and subversive actions ultimately the monks evict Remigius from the priory effectively turning Remigius into a beggar. Sometime later Phillip encounters a sickly and impoverished Remigius. Remigius begs forgiveness. Phillip does forgive but takes a further step, placing the ailing Remigius on his donkey to ride while Phillips walks beside him, on-foot back to Kingsbridge. This is the spirit of forgiveness and restoration that marked the life of Joseph; the willingness to be larger than others and larger than their offense; large enough to forgive, large enough to engender restoration if restoration was possible.

Forgiveness is always possible even if restoration is not. There is no magic to the matter; if we forgive it does not necessarily follow that the offender will repent, see the error of his or her ways. Forgiveness frees us from the actions of another. Forgiveness frees us to act freely; it opens the door to any self-imposed prison of hatred, resentment and anger. We forgive because we are forgiven. We forgive because as Christians we know that God is in all events working them for our ultimate good. The offender may wield their evil tool as an act of malice to wound, but that evil tool becomes a scalpel in the hand of God to perform surgery on our heart and soul. The incision wounds, but what the enemy would use to destroy our great God uses to build the character of His son Jesus in our lives. Just as God was with Joseph, so He is with us.

CHAPTER THIRTY-EIGHT

MAGNUM OPUS

This book addresses both those who are currently suffering and those who have suffered. Suffering produces impatience with triteness and flippant answers to hard deep questions. Those who suffer lose patience with nice churches with answers to nice questions. The fierceness of emotional and/or physical pain focuses our souls to issues that are precise and answers that are cogent; we want serious, well considered answers to very difficult questions.

Serious faith desires and needs a declaration of a God who is here, who rules and is involved. Serious faith points to a complex God who is both present and yet also infinite and unknowably wise. We long for a faith in a God who is good; but goodness that goes beyond niceness or softness. We need a goodness that makes sense of pain and suffering and does not relegate God to a character of useless and powerless affability. The God we look for is not a genial old man who has no firm opinions, no standards or boundaries. Rather, we look for the God triune; we look for the son who is represented as the lion Aslan in CS Lewis' Chronicles of Narnia. This God-man represented by a majestic and terrible lion, is not safe, or tame. He is great and powerful and majestic; as Lewis describes Aslan, he is not safe. Infinitely wise and loving he is also strong.

This Jesus is the God that we see and need when we're in times of trouble. We desperately need a God who is sovereign and immutable, a God who is omnipotent. We need a God who is good; the King of all the earth who does what is right. It is when we have this God, the very God revealed in Scripture's that in the midst of great suffering we can rest in his character. We can know He is doing what is right and good, ultimately for our lives, for the world and for His own glory.

Joni Eareckson Tada says her best healing has been in the wheelchair—healing of heart and soul. Sometimes our greatest healing comes from a denial of our most heart-felt desire, a changing of our will into greater compliance with God's will, greater submission. Did Joseph ask God for a release from the prison during those two additional years in jail? Did he ask often? God's answer was "No, Joseph, the time is not right-not yet."

In the narrative that is Joseph's life in this book as well as the narrative we have of Ruth in the Old Testament book of her name, we see two lives that endured great suffering and heartache. Ruth's suffering was a result of living in a fallen world; Joseph suffered at the hands of men. Yet for all of their suffering, they endured and ultimately they triumphed over that suffering with a joyful and positive resolution to their life dilemmas. The lives of both Joseph and Ruth ended on a note of victory but for those of us who suffer in this life, and indeed we all do, that victory may be in question here, even seemingly delayed. There seems to be much unknown, as many questions, if not more, as there are answers and there is a sense of disquiet and unease.

By way of contemporary pop-culture example the lives of Joseph and Ruth can be likened to the scenario of the film, Star Wars where there is destruction of the enemy's main weapon and the ending is one of jubilation. Yet for many of us our lives are like the ending of Star Wars: The Empire Strikes Back, the sequel where the enemy has made more advances and seemingly triumphed and the whole issue is still yet in question, issues yet resolved. These two fictional scenarios are somewhat (but not perfectly by any means) analogous to our lives. Sometimes hope for victory is deferred sometimes victory seems fleeting. Sometimes victory must wait for the life to come.

As much as possible I have avoided using the personal pronoun "I" in this book. It is not merely a matter of style but also a move of substance. The focus of all of this is God and the truth of God for our lives as conveyed in the life of Joseph. But now, I will pull the cover back again and be a little more personal for reasons of our discussion.

I think of my wife Anna, who for some years now has been struggling with painful back and sciatic issues. Over the years she has been to various doctors, she has tried different treatments and although there has been some improvement, major issues of pain are still not resolved. Earlier this year, a firm diagnosis was finally made as that of Spondylolisthesis. I look into my own life with health issues related to simply aging and then issues of disease and it is painful to consider that my life shows the veracity of Scripture where it says that our bodies are wasting away. Yet we hold on with hope, as the verse tells us, that our spiritual being is renewed day by day. The body is wasting away, the body is dying and each day I come closer to that day where I will slip this tent, this earthly dwelling and go to an eternal one.

We can reasonably ask the question: where is God's care and Providence in the struggles that do not relent. The sciatic pain continues for my wife, perhaps for another person their second heart attack is fatal or for a child with cystic fibrosis one day they take their last breath. We cannot adopt a theology that sweeps away these very real issues, issues that seemingly, are without quick or easy answer, certainly in the individual cases. There is an over-arching reason that can be discovered in the person of God.

What is God doing; what is His purpose? We must come to the realization if we are to have any peace and keep our sanity, that there is ambiguity in our current existence. All questions will not be answered here. Suffering and injustice do remain.

Solomon sought to explain the mysteries of life; he pronounced all of life as vanity or futility, we will not. As we said at the beginning of the book God is not a Deist. God is involved in all of history He is the grand conductor of a celestial orchestra and He is bringing his magnum opus to a finale. Each instrument (us) sight reads the musical piece that is before us and we have our own heart for our individual instrument. Our music does not drown out the melody and counter melodies and movements of music around us played around us by other chairs and other instruments. We do not have before us, however, a complete score of all the parts. Since we are sight reading we do not necessarily know beyond a very basic shadow of an idea where all of this is heading. The conductor (God) however, does have the complete score indeed He is not only the conductor He is the composer and He knows each part intimately well. The conductor knows each instrument. He knows the flow of the parts to the climax of the individual parts in the entire musical composition.

Joseph, his father and his brothers all played their part in the musical piece that is the book of Genesis. Their individual instruments blended into one musical composition. The conductor used the dissonance of favoritism and jealousy, pride and humility rage and even hatred to create a melody of trust, of faithfulness, of repentance and peace.

We cannot in our finiteness answer the question for each and every individual; we can state that the mysteries to us are known to God. But we can move to a theodicy, where we reasonably defend the goodness of God in the face of uncertain or hard circumstances. We can state that as God was with Joseph even in his most dire of circumstances God is with us even in our most dire of moments. He is for us. In the midst of any suffering in any trial any questions of life and any ambiguities we must go back to the truth that God is for us and our ultimate good.

We can state that God is for us and that all of the answers to all of the questions of this life are bound up in the glory of God. The purpose of creation of which we are a part is to bring glory to Yahweh God. The universe is God's grand symphony; it is His magnum opus.

THE END

ABOUT THE AUTHOR

B rian Bailey lives and writes in Florida. He is a faculty member of Tallahassee Christian College and Training Center. A teacher by education, Brian also has thirty years experience in the public and private sector. Joseph: A Life of Providence, Injustice, and Forgiveness, is his fifth book.

Please follow Brian on Facebook at
ThreshingFloorMinistry.com

****

OTHER BOOKS BY BRIAN BAILEY

RUTH: A GUIDE FOR LIFE'S TROUBLED TIMES

A GREAT CLOUD (A GREAT CLOUD OF WITNESSES)

SACRED TREASURES: BROKEN CLAY—GRACE IN THE EXTREME

WHY NARNIA MATTERS (A GREAT CLOUD OF WITNESSES, VOLUME 2)